DUNG
FOR DINNER

A Stomach-Churning Look at the
Animal Poop, Pee, Vomit, and Secretions
That People Have Eaten (and Often Still Do!)

CHRISTINE VIRNIG

ILLUSTRATED BY KORWIN BRIGGS

GODWINBOOKS

HENRY HOLT AND COMPANY

NEW YORK

To Sam and Rachel, for enduring the embarrassment
of having a mom who writes about poop

Henry Holt and Company, *Publishers since 1866*
Henry Holt® is a registered trademark of Macmillan Publishing Group, LLC
120 Broadway, New York, NY 10271 • mackids.com

Text copyright © 2020 by Christine Virnig
Illustrations copyright © 2020 by Korwin Briggs
All rights reserved.

ISBN 978-1-250-24679-0

Library of Congress Control Number: 2019949983

Our books may be purchased in bulk for promotional, educational, or business
use. Please contact your local bookseller or the Macmillan Corporate and
Premium Sales Department at (800) 221-7945 ext. 5442 or by email at
MacmillanSpecialMarkets@macmillan.com.

First edition, 2020 / Designed by Liz Dresner
Printed in the United States of America by LSC Communications,
Harrisonburg, Virginia

1 3 5 7 9 10 8 6 4 2

CONTENTS

FOREWORD

YOU PROBABLY THINK animal poop and pee are disgusting. It's hard not to when you consider Fluffy's malodorous litter box. Or the pungent stench of cow manure that greets your nose when you drive through farm country. And let's not forget all those Fido poop piles you have to pick up with a plastic bag whenever you take him for a walk.

But believe it or not, animal poop, pee, vomit, and secretions are not all bad. They can be used for all sorts of remarkable things.

For thousands of years people around the world have built homes out of dried animal dung.

During the nineteenth century an important ingredient in gunpowder was pee.

Need some new boots? If you lived during the Victorian era, the boot's leather would have been processed using pigeon poo.

Even today lots of lotions, moisturizers, and lip balms contain lanolin, which is a waxy secretion made by sheep.

Animal poop is also sometimes used for fun. If you live in the cheesehead state of Wisconsin, as I do, you might already know that cow poop isn't only used as a fertilizer around here. The small village of Prairie du Sac has a cow chip–throwing festival every year. The main attraction is watching grown-ups compete to see who can chuck a dried-out disc of cow dung the farthest. (In case you're wondering, the longest toss ever recorded at the festival was a whopping 248 feet—which is about the length of thirty cows standing in a line!)

There are so many good uses for poop and pee and secretions that an entire book could be written on the subject.

This is not that book.

In this book we're going to forget that animal dung can be a cooking fuel and that pee was once used to clean clothes. Instead, we're going to focus on the animal poop, pee, vomit, and secretions that people *put in their mouths*. Because that's way more fun. And way more gross.

Speaking of "gross," as you read through the chapters and (hopefully!) find yourself feeling disgusted from time to time, keep in mind that your "Ew!" might be another person's "Yum!" A prized delicacy in one part of the world can be considered revolting to people living elsewhere. And things that were perfectly normal to see in a medicine cabinet at one point in history can become repulsive with the passing of time.

Just think . . . there are undoubtedly things *you* regularly chow down on that would make a person living in a different country, or in a different era, want to hurl. Like maybe meat loaf. Or American cheese. Or tuna fish casserole. Or chocolate chip cookies.

(I'm obviously joking about the last one. Nobody could ever find chocolate chip cookies repulsive. Could they?)

A WARNING!

AS YOU'VE PROBABLY figured out, this book is about gross things people eat. Things like animal poop. And pee. And vomit. And secretions.

Our human history is chock-full of people who have eaten stuff like this. And those "people"? They include you!

Yes . . . *you!*

Read this book and you'll soon discover some rather shocking things about your food. It might even make you think twice the next time someone hands you a bag of candy corn.

With that in mind, before turning the page, stop and think for a minute. Does the idea of eating insect vomit or bird spit make your stomach squirm?

If so, maybe put this book back on the shelf and choose something different. Like a book about fluffy little bunny rabbits. (Consider yourself warned: Bunny rabbits eat poop, too.)

But if eating whale poop doesn't bother you at all, go

ahead and turn the page! Unless you're eating, of course. If you're eating, please close this book, finish your lunch, and come back later.

> ### Some quick legal mumbo jumbo:
>
> Just because this book discusses eating camel poop and ox snot and astronaut pee, this *does not mean* you should go out and chow down on camel poop or ox snot or astronaut pee. This book is meant to be fun and gross and hopefully a bit educational. It is *not* meant to be a recipe book or a medical handbook.

PART 1

HEALTH & MEDICINE

Poop, pee, vomit, and secretions
that people have scarfed down
(and sometimes still do!)
in the name of health

1

Tylenol à la Boar Dung

Wild boar, with their hairy pig bodies and pointy tusks, look terrifying. You sure wouldn't want to run into one on the street. You also wouldn't want to run into their poop on the street. Wild boar dung reeks! There is nothing appetizing about it. And yet the ancient Romans chose to consume it. But why?

While we'll never know exactly what was going through the mind of that first excrement-ingesting pioneer, we do know that Roman charioteers were the boar poop–guzzling champions of ancient Rome. And the reason the charioteers chose to eat it was rather . . . interesting.

Charioteers were the heroes of the most popular spectator sport in ancient Rome: chariot racing. Chariot racing was basically the great-great-great-great-grandfather of NASCAR. Except instead of sitting in a car while racing around a track, the drivers (or charioteers) balanced on lightweight wooden carts pulled by teams of horses.

While many charioteers were enslaved, this wasn't true for all of them. Charioteers who won loads of races could become exceedingly rich. They were treated like celebrities. The public adored them.

But before you start yearning for your own shot at charioteer glory, there is something you should know. Chariot racing was extremely dangerous. Imagine twelve chariots hurtling around a narrow track at the same time. Hooves pound against the ground, stirring up dust, as sweaty charioteers whip their horses to ever greater speeds.

As the chariots barreled around the tight corners, spectacular, life-ending collisions were common. Even if charioteers avoided a crash, they could still be thrown from their chariot and end up dragged by their horses, trampled by hooves, or run over by a wheel.

Peacock Brains, Anyone?

Exotic ingredients didn't only show up in ancient Roman medicine. Rich Romans also liked to *eat* all kinds of outlandish things. Peacock brains. Flamingo tongues. Dormice. And lucky for them, if eating peacock brains left them with bad breath, they knew just how to fix it. Burn some mouse droppings, mix the ashes with honey, smear the concoction all over their teeth, and bye-bye, bad breath!

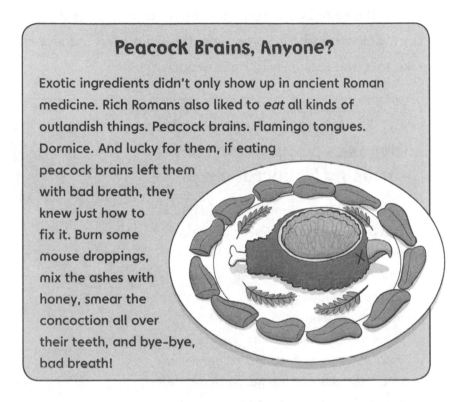

At the end of a race, charioteers often found themselves in anything but pristine condition. Colorful bruises. Broken bones. Gaping wounds. A pounding headache. The pain these charioteers felt would have made any normal person reach for a bottle of extra-strength Tylenol.

But alas . . . Tylenol wouldn't be invented until 1955, so it wasn't exactly an option for an ancient Roman living two thousand years ago. There was also no Walgreens. No Superman Band-Aids. No penguin-shaped ice packs.

So the poor battered charioteers had to be resourceful and look around for something they *did* have access to. Like lots and lots of wild boar droppings.

Emperor Nero: Olympic Champion or Poop-Drinking Embarrassment?

Nero, Roman emperor from 54 to 68 CE, was apparently a big fan of drinking dung. This was likely because Nero— much to the embarrassment of his advisers—had charioteer ambitions of his own. He even took time off from some of his other pursuits, such as murdering his mother and killing his wife, to drive a team of ten horses in a chariot race during the Olympic games. And he won! Well . . . technically Nero fell out of his chariot and never crossed the finish line, but when you're emperor, apparently something as trivial as finishing a race is no obstacle to Olympic glory.

6

At some point a desperate, achy charioteer probably looked at a fresh pile of dung and thought, "Hmm, I wonder . . . ," and the rest is history.

According to the ancient Roman author Pliny the Elder, the way the poop was prepared depended on the injury a person was dealing with.

If bruises were your problem, you wanted wild boar dung that had been collected in the spring and dried.

If you'd been "dragged by a chariot or lacerated by the wheels," the boar dung could be used fresh, dried, or boiled in vinegar.

Fractured ribs? For this you actually wanted *goat* excrement mixed with "old wine."

And for painful tendons or ligaments, goat droppings boiled in vinegar and honey was the way to go.

Some charioteers undoubtedly lathered the poop mixtures right on their bumps and bruises. Like slathering aloe on a sunburn, except with a slightly more off-putting aroma.

Those charioteers who really wanted to get the job done right didn't settle for merely spreading feces on their skin, though. No sirree. They *drank* the poop-y concoctions!

Tylenol à la Boar Dung!

Guzzling Boar Dung Was Only the Beginning

HURRY!

The ancient Roman author Pliny the Elder didn't only write about boar dung. In his book, *The Natural History*, he wrote about a whole host of interesting medical treatments. Human earwax could be smeared on snake bites and scorpion stings. Camel brains— after being dried and mixed with vinegar— treated seizures. Wolf dung could be applied to treat cataracts. And the best remedy for asthma? Drink wild horse blood!

ALMOST GOT IT!

SQUEAK SQUEAK

Q: How can you tell who lost the chariot race?

A: Just look for the chariot tears!

The Ancient Romans Were Not Alone!

It's easy to look back at the ancient Romans and wonder, "What on earth were they thinking?" How could they believe drinking boar dung would cure *anything*? But if you jumped into a time machine and traveled two thousand years into the future, undoubtedly people will be asking "What on earth were they thinking?" about all kinds of things that seem perfectly normal to us today.

Furthermore, odd-sounding cures showed up all around the ancient world. Doctors in ancient Egypt, for example, used crocodile poop. And ancient Chinese medicine was jam-packed with interesting ingredients like dandruff, spiderwebs, human hair, stained underwear . . . and a whole lot of poop, pee, saliva, and snot.

Here is a taste of some treatments used in ancient Chinese herbal medicine:

- Have a bad case of BO (i.e., your armpits smell like a combination of sour milk, rotten eggs, and maggoty fish)? Try washing your pits in your own pee several times a day.
- Bit by a snake? Eat some flying squirrel dung.
- Find yourself choking on a bone? Drip dog saliva down your throat.
- Run across a frightened, convulsing infant? Collect some ox snot, mix it with water, and force-feed it to the baby.

After reading about the various treatments used by the ancient Romans, Egyptians, and Chinese, you're probably feeling relieved to be living in the twenty-first century. Except . . . surprise! Poop still shows up in medicine today. And you'll learn all about it in Chapter 7!

2

Eat Poop to Stop Pooping

PHRRT

There is no doubt about it: Diarrhea stinks. (In more ways than one!) But imagine trying to *fight a war* while being plagued with a bad case of the runs. Louis IX—the king of France from 1226 to 1270—faced just this problem while he was off leading the Seventh Crusade. His diarrhea got so bad, in fact, that when he felt the urge to go, he had a hard time getting his pants down fast enough. His solution? He cut a hole right in the back of his breeches!

This wartime diarrhea is usually called dysentery. Which is a fancy name for an infection—from a bacteria, a virus, or a parasite—that causes a person to get bloody diarrhea, often along with severe stomachaches, high fevers, and nausea.

As you might imagine, a puking, pooping, high-fevered person simply doesn't make the best soldier. Think back to the last time *you* had the stomach flu. Do you remember how weak and exhausted you felt? Now imagine you had to pick up a sword, or a gun, and fight for your life. Odds are, it would not be pretty.

Worse than having a slew of sick, dehydrated soldiers lying about was having no soldiers at all. Because dysentery killed people! Remember our friend King "hole-in-his-breeches" Louis IX? He might have survived his bout with diarrhea during the Seventh Crusade, but his father wasn't so lucky. He got dysentery on his way home from fighting in the Albigensian Crusade, and it killed him. And during the American Civil War? Dysentery was blamed for the deaths of tens of thousands of soldiers!

Deadly Diarrhea

Diarrhea is awful. Simply awful. As miserable as we feel when we've got the runs, though, most of us don't fear *dying* because of it. Diarrhea isn't the same as meningitis or brain cancer or heart attacks; it doesn't kill people nowadays as it did back during the Civil War. Or does it?

Sadly, yes. Diarrhea does still kill.

A big part of the problem is that lots of people around the world, at least two *billion*, get their drinking water from sources contaminated with poop. And this tainted water is estimated to cause about five hundred thousand diarrheal deaths a year!

Fast forward to World War II, and wartime dysentery was still a major problem. Just ask the German soldiers stationed in Africa. Instead of fighting the Allies, they began spending more and more time camped on the toilet. It became such a serious problem that the German medical corps was called in.

Exploding Dung

Amazingly, camel dung's role as a health miracle was not its sole claim to fame during World War II. For some reason, German tank drivers believed driving over camel dung would bring them good luck. So whenever they saw a poop pile, they purposely steered over it.

The Allies saw this behavior and had a light bulb moment. They began making explosives that looked like camel poop. Then some poor, unsuspecting German would see the fake dung heap, steer his tank over it, and *BOOM!* No more tank.

It didn't take long before the Germans figured out what was going on, and they stopped seeking out untouched poop. Instead, they drove over camel poop that had already been run over—figuring this was a sure sign the poo was safe. But alas for the Germans, the Allies were one step ahead of them again.

The Allies had started making bombs that looked like already-flattened camel dung!

Then the Germans noticed something odd. Whenever the local Bedouin people began developing symptoms of dysentery, they recovered super fast. *They* weren't suffering from unrelenting diarrhea. *They* weren't plagued by excruciating stomach pains. *They* weren't dying left and right. What was their secret?

The Germans did some investigating and discovered something astonishing. Whenever one of the locals began feeling queasy, he'd follow his camel around. He'd follow it and follow it and follow it until eventually the camel pooped out a big stinky pile of droppings. What happened next? He would bend down, scoop up a steaming turd, and eat it!

After observing this peculiar behavior, the German medical corps figured they'd better start studying camel dung. Before long, it became clear that the Bedouin people were really on to something, because fresh camel poo was teeming with a remarkably hungry bacteria called *Bacillus subtilis*, which was basically a virus-and-bacteria-gobbling machine. So whenever an army of *Bacillus subtilis* traveled through a person's gut, it devoured everything in its path—including the mischievous, dysentery-causing germ.

Which meant?

No more dysentery!

Fresh Is Best

The Bedouin people followed their camels around, waiting for fresh poo to eat, because ingesting camel dung only cured dysentery if it was still warm. As soon as the poop cooled, all the little *Bacillus subtilis* died. And a dead bacteria simply can't do much devouring.

GENUINE CAMEL DUNG

GET 'EM WHILE THEY'RE HOT!

Lucky for the German soldiers, the medical corps found a way for them to get the benefits of eating fresh, steaming camel poop without needing to actually eat fresh, steaming camel poop. They did this by making huge vats of *Bacillus subtilis* and having the soldiers slurp that down instead.

Q: How do we know that King Louis IX's diarrhea
was hereditary?

A: It ran in his genes!

Camel Poo Power

Camel poop's contribution to humanity doesn't start or end with World War II. For much of human history, animal dung, including camel droppings, has been used as a cooking fuel.

And recently, smart people in the United Arab Emirates have come up with a powerful new way to utilize camel dung. By mixing the poop with wood and trash, they can make electricity! In fact, several cement factories already use this poo power successfully.

What a marvelous way to get rid of pesky poop piles, preserve natural resources, and reduce landfill waste, all at the same time!

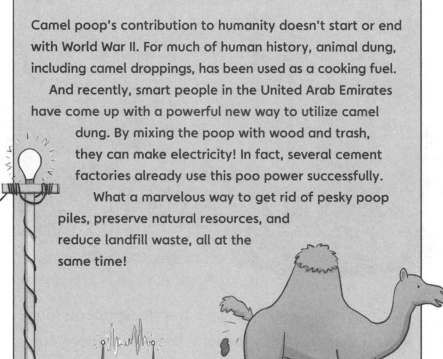

3

Doctors Used to Taste _What?_

Before we start this chapter, I'm going to let you in on a little secret. I'm a doctor. An MD. A physician. And in my role as a doc, I get to deal with all kinds of things that most people find disgusting. I've stuck needles here and inserted tubes there. I've been coughed on, puked on, and bled on. I've had sick toddlers sneeze snot rockets at me way more times than I care to count.

To be honest, none of these things bother me much. I consider it part of the job. But when I was researching this chapter—and was reading about what physicians used to do? Well . . . let's just say it made me exceedingly happy to be practicing medicine today.

In many ways, doctors nowadays have it made. When faced with a sick patient, we can order a slew of tests in hopes of finding the cause. We can do skin tests to look for allergies, draw blood to look for thyroid problems, swab a throat to look for strep, and even peer inside bodies—without cutting them open!—by using CT scanners and MRI machines.

The ancient Greeks living thousands of years ago had none of that. They had no way of knowing that Aunt Marge's cough was caused by a virus or that Big John was vomiting because he ate raw chicken or that Suzy's stomach hurt because her appendix was minutes away from bursting.

So not knowing what actually caused disease, the ancient Greeks did what humans often do when faced with the unknown: They blamed the gods. They figured the gods could rain illnesses down upon the Earth whenever they pleased—out of anger, as a punishment, or out of sheer boredom.

And how does one "cure" a disease caused by the gods? By asking the gods for help, of course.

The Greeks usually turned to Asclepius, the god of medicine. They built temples in his name all over the ancient Greek world, and sick people traveled far and wide to reach one. After arriving at a temple, they'd go through a cleansing ritual, then spend the night inside. A little snooze sounds pleasant enough . . . except for the snakes. Snakes were sacred to Asclepius, so they were welcome guests in his temples. They slithered across the floor, weaving their way among the sleepers, licking at wounds.

In the morning, the patients would wake up and tell their dreams to a priest, who would interpret them. With any luck, the dreams would suggest a treatment—a prayer, a sacrifice, a charm, a diet—that would bring about a cure.

This focus on the gods as the cause, and the cure, for sickness changed with the appearance of one particular physician: Hippocrates. Born around 460 BCE on the island of Cos, Hippocrates would eventually be known as the father of medicine. He and his followers took the gods right out of the disease-causing business. Instead, they believed all diseases had a natural cause; the gods had nothing to do with it.

This meant a clever doctor could now strive to *understand* diseases. To discover the cause, to predict what would happen next, and hopefully to find a cure.

19

The Life of a God Is Not All That

So who was this Asclepius guy who had healing temples all over ancient Greece? What was his story? While Asclepius has been given the title god of medicine, his status as a true god is somewhat murky. His father was a god, but his mother was a mere human. And he was mortal—like you and me. Despite this, he was worshipped like a god by people throughout the ancient world.

Just as his god–not god status was fuzzy, so too was his life story. Every version you read tells a slightly different tale—all of which are disturbing. Here is one account.

Asclepius's father was Apollo, the god of music. One day Apollo became infatuated with Coronis, a human princess, and she became pregnant with Asclepius. Before she gave birth, though, Coronis had the nerve to fall in love with someone else. As you can imagine, Apollo was sad and heartbroken and furious. So Apollo's sister sought revenge for her jilted brother by killing the pregnant Coronis.

Things sure weren't looking very bright for Asclepius at that point, but he was lucky. The winged god Hermes swooped down and rescued Asclepius before he could die along with his mother.

Asclepius was given to Chiron to raise. Chiron was a centaur, half horse and half human. While most centaurs were wild and lawless, Chiron was not. He was kind and smart. He happily taught Asclepius all about healing. Asclepius was a great student, and before long he had become a healing master. He got so good, in fact, that he figured out how to bring people back from the dead.

This might sound awesome, but Hades didn't like it. Hades was the god of the underworld, and Asclepius's heroics were depriving him of souls. Zeus—the king of the gods—also didn't think too much of Asclepius's talent. If humans could cheat death, they would practically be gods themselves. That couldn't be allowed. So Zeus did what anyone in his position would have done: He killed Asclepius with a lightning bolt.

Now considering Apollo had been a fairly distant father throughout Asclepius's life, one would think he'd shrug off the whole my-son-got-vaporized-by-the-king-of-the-gods thing. But he didn't. He was royally miffed off. He decided to get even.

Apollo couldn't exactly kill Zeus, who was his father *and* the head god dude.

So instead, he killed the Cyclopes. Because they had invented Zeus's lightning bolt.

The one bright spot in this whole sad tale was that Zeus eventually felt guilty for pulverizing Asclepius. So he turned Asclepius into the constellation Ophiucus, the Serpent Bearer.

To learn more, physicians started analyzing their patients like crazy. They left no stone unturned as they labored to discover the secrets behind illness. Because they didn't have X-rays or petri dishes or fancy lab tests, they relied on what they did have: five senses.

Hippocratic Corpus or Just Corpus?

Until recently, Hippocrates was given credit for writing a whole host of medical papers. They were even named after him: the Hippocratic Corpus. Now we're almost certain Hippocrates didn't write the whole thing. In fact, he might not have written any of it!

They used their eyes to see. What did a patient's skin look like? If a urine sample was obtained, what color was the pee? If a wound was oozing pus, what did the pus look like? The physicians even took note of patients' eye color, hair texture, and whether they ground their teeth (which was a sure sign of madness).

Physicians used their ears to listen. How did a patient's cough sound? Did the patient speak with a lisp? (They believed lisps made a person more prone to diarrhea.)

They even listened to a patient's belches and took note of whether farts were quiet or loud!

They used their fingers to touch. Did a patient have cold ears, dry skin, or sticky sweat? What did phlegm feel like? What did poop feel like?

They used their nose to smell. They smelled pus. They smelled vomit. They even smelled poo.

And finally . . . they used their tongue to taste. And they tasted e-v-e-r-y-t-h-i-n-g. If a patient was coughing up bloody phlegm . . . taste it. A snotty nose? Taste the boogers. Pee a bit cloudy? You guessed it. Taste it. It was believed that the best way to know what was going on *inside* a person was to study what was coming *out* of the person, *so* how those bodily fluids tasted was thought to be super important.

The Death of George Washington

Around Hippocrates's time, patients were often treated by getting rid of "excess fluids." The theory was that people got sick because their body was out of balance, and by making them puke or poop or bleed, everything would return to normal, and they'd be cured.

Of these options, puking and pooping were certainly the smelliest. But bleeding—also called bloodletting—was the most popular. And it was done *a lot*.

Unfortunately, the concept of bloodletting didn't die with Hippocrates and his immediate successors. During the Middle Ages, if you were feeling a bit off, you could simply head to your local barbershop. There your beard-trimming, hair-cutting barber could cut your arm and extract some blood.

Move on to the eighteenth century, and bloodletting was still widespread. In fact, many people blame George Washington's death on overenthusiastic bleeding.

Washington's downfall started with a simple sore throat, but that night his breathing became labored. Three doctors were summoned the next day. They held nothing back as they worked desperately to help the beloved first president. During his final day on earth, Washington was given an enema to make him poo, an emetic to make him vomit, and he was bled *four* times. In total, more than eighty ounces of his precious blood were removed. That's enough to fill more than six cans of Coke!

If you ever feel like channeling *your* inner Hippocrates, the next time you're feeling under the weather, collect some of your earwax and give it a lick. If it tastes bitter, according to ancient beliefs, you can breathe a sigh of relief. Chances are you'll recover. But if your earwax tastes sweet? Watch out! Death could be right around the corner.[1]*

Q: If you lived in ancient Greece, would an apple a day keep the doctor away?

A: Only if you aimed well enough!

Earwax Candles?

Hippocrates might have tasted earwax, but Shrek— the large, green, princess-marrying, swamp-dwelling ogre—makes candles out of his earwax.

Can this really be done? To find out, the crew from the TV show *MythBusters* attempted to do just that. And they discovered the answer was . . . no. Earwax cannot be made into a functioning candle. To be fair, though, they did use *human* earwax in their experiment. Perhaps the key to making an earwax candle is finding *ogre* earwax.

1   * FYI: *Do not* actually taste your earwax to determine whether you will live or die.

Pearly White Pearly Whites

Now it's time to head back to ancient Rome, because guzzling wild boar dung wasn't the only gross thing the Romans did. But before we pick on them yet again, let's first stop and recall that ancient Rome wasn't all bad. The Romans did some amazing things.

- They built incredible monuments, like the Colosseum and the Pantheon.
- They left a network of paved roads that crisscrossed the Roman Empire. These roads allowed for the easier transportation of people, goods, and armies.
- They built a complex sewer system and constructed huge aqueducts to supply cities and fields with water.

Considering all these great achievements in architecture and civil engineering, it's no wonder the ancient Romans also sought solutions for their other problems. Like how to turn a mouthful of yellow teeth into something dazzlingly white.

They couldn't simply wander down to the local pharmacy and buy tooth-whitening strips; life wasn't that easy. But somewhere along the line, a smart Roman discovered that ammonia could be used to whiten teeth. And woo-hoo! Blindingly white smile, here we come.

Wait a second, though. Where did they get the ammonia?

Did they get it from vegetable matter?

Nope.

Did they invent a sophisticated way to isolate the trace amounts of ammonia found in seawater?

Nope.

Did they build a rocket ship, blast off into space, high-tail it to Jupiter, and capture an ammonia cloud?

Wrong again.

The ancient Romans opted to get their ammonia from a much more convenient place: pee. Stale *human* pee to be exact.

Extra! Extra! Read All About It!
Father of Modern Dentistry Endorses Pee!

Pierre Fauchard, often considered the father of modern dentistry, had one thing in common with the ancient Romans. He might have been practicing in the 1700s—at a time when ancient Rome was already ancient history—but he also recommended urine as a treatment. Instead of using pee to whiten teeth, though, he recommended gargling with urine twice a day as a remedy for toothaches!

New Dung Times

PIERRE FAUCHARD
GARGLES PEE-PEE

POTTY?   URINE TROUBLE

Luckily for a yellow-toothed Roman, human pee wasn't hard to come by. Even though they did have a complex sewer system, they didn't have flush toilets. So their pee wasn't getting whooshed away, never to be seen (or gargled) again.

Nope. Pee was abundant because lots of full-bladdered Romans used a chamber pot—basically a bowl that served as a portable toilet. You could keep it in your house or take it on the road with you. If you were wealthy enough, you might even have an enslaved person whose glamorous job was to follow you around and carry your toilet.

Once a chamber pot was full, the contents were supposed to be poured into a sewer drain, but this didn't always happen. It was much less work to dump everything out a window. As you might imagine, there were rules prohibiting this kind of thing, but those rules weren't obeyed any better than you obey your mom when she tells you to clean your room. Needless to say, an umbrella could come in handy when walking through ancient Roman cities, what with the ever-present threat of pee raining down upon you.

But instead of dumping the urine onto a neighbor's head, that full chamber pot could be considered a nice bowl of tooth-whitening magic.

For an ancient Roman who didn't have a chamber pot to pee in, another option was to find a street corner. Evidence suggests many cities had terra-cotta pots sitting out on street corners to serve as peeing spots. These pots often leaked or broke open—undoubtedly leaving a smelly mess on the street. But when they remained intact? Ta-da! You had another great source of pearly white–making mouthwash.

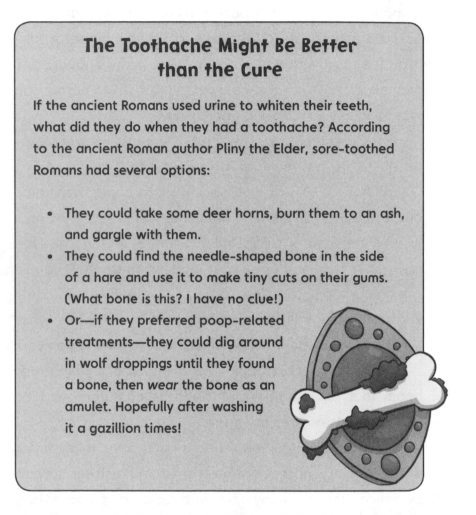

The Toothache Might Be Better than the Cure

If the ancient Romans used urine to whiten their teeth, what did they do when they had a toothache? According to the ancient Roman author Pliny the Elder, sore-toothed Romans had several options:

- They could take some deer horns, burn them to an ash, and gargle with them.
- They could find the needle-shaped bone in the side of a hare and use it to make tiny cuts on their gums. (What bone is this? I have no clue!)
- Or—if they preferred poop-related treatments—they could dig around in wolf droppings until they found a bone, then *wear* the bone as an amulet. Hopefully after washing it a gazillion times!

What would first-century Roman physicians think of all this? They'd probably advise against using any old chamber-pot pee. And they'd most likely recommend against run-of-the-mill street corner pee as well.

Instead, they apparently preferred imported pee— ideally from Portugal!

Q: Why couldn't the ancient Roman fix his loose tooth?
A: Toothpaste hadn't been invented yet!

The Joys of Pooping in Ancient Rome

Exploding Toilets!

If you were an ancient Roman, chamber pots and street corners weren't the only places you could do your business. You could also use a communal toilet. These toilets were basically buildings full of long benches with holes carved into them. To use one, you'd simply yank up your toga, sit over a hole, and *drip, drip, plop, plop*.

A communal toilet might have a few seats, or it could have more than a hundred. Because there were no partitions between the seats, you could be doing your thing over one hole while someone else sat a foot away doing their thing.

To me, communal toilets make Porta Potties seem downright heavenly. But some historians (not all of them!) think the ancient Romans used public toilets as a place to socialize. Whether you were a rich Roman running for political office, a poor Roman wanting to gossip about the neighbors, or a sewer rat wanting to be around poop, a communal toilet may have been the place to be. The poet Martial even writes about a man who hung out in public toilets hoping to get a dinner invitation, but this may have been an exaggeration.

For those who ventured into the communal toilets—whether to make friends or simply to go number two—there was always potential for excitement. Not only did the lack of sewer traps mean that vermin—such as sewer rats—were frequently popping up to say hello, but on a trip to a communal toilet you might get treated to a fireworks show. Methane and hydrogen sulfide would build up in the sewers running under the toilets. Occasionally the gas would ignite. And *BOOM!* Exploding toilets.

Ancient Roman Toilet Paper

Communal toilets probably don't seem all that appealing. You've got no privacy. You've got sewer rats. You've got exploding toilets. You've got a smell that must have been out of this world. But there's something about communal toilets that most of us would agree was even worse: the *xylospongium*.

Ancient Romans hadn't invented ultraplush, two-ply toilet paper yet, so some historians believe they used a *xylospongium* instead. What's a *xylospongium*, you ask? It's a sponge. Attached to the end of a stick.

Here is the idea: When you were all done pooping, you'd grab a *xylospongium* and use it to clean your you-know-what. After you were done you'd give the sponge—now coated in (insert your name here) dung—a quick rinse. Then you'd leave it for the next person to use!

So HOW ABOUT THAT WEATHER?

please rinse after using.

5

Sweet, Sweet Pee

By now you know all about Hippocrates. How he and his fellow physicians were listening to farts, smelling vomit, and tasting earwax. But Hippocrates was born around 460 BCE. That was before Cleopatra reigned. Before the Incans built Machu Picchu. And over a thousand years before

Islam become a religion. In other words, Hippocrates lived a long, long, *long* time ago.

Now fast-forward to the Middle Ages—about fifteen hundred years after Hippocrates. Surely doctors were more sophisticated about how they diagnosed diseases.

Or maybe not. Because in the Middle Ages, doctoring was all about the pee.

Yup. The pee.

Don't believe me? Look at a painting of a physician during the Middle Ages, and there is one thing you will almost always see: a flask of urine. More than likely, the doctor will be holding the flask up to the light while gazing intently at the yellowish liquid contained within. It's as if the doctor thought the liquid held all the answers.

Odds are, he *did* think the liquid held all the answers. Uroscopy is the fancy name for what the doctor was doing— diagnosing medical problems by studying a patient's urine. The doc would take note of the urine's color. Was it yellow? Brown? Red? Black? Orange? Was the pee cloudy or clear? If the pee sat for a while, would there be any sediment? If the doctor took a sip, how did the urine taste?

After studying any given urine sample, the physician would consult his urine chart. These charts were handmade drawings typically showing at least twenty possible variations on how a person's pee might look. The doctor would pick the closest match, and ta-da! The chart would tell him all he needed to know about what was wrong with the patient.

Testing the Tester

As physicians during the Middle Ages depended more and more on pee analysis, others wanted in on the action. After all, with the help of a urine chart, anyone could make a diagnosis, including a worker at the local apothecary . . . or a traveling quack.

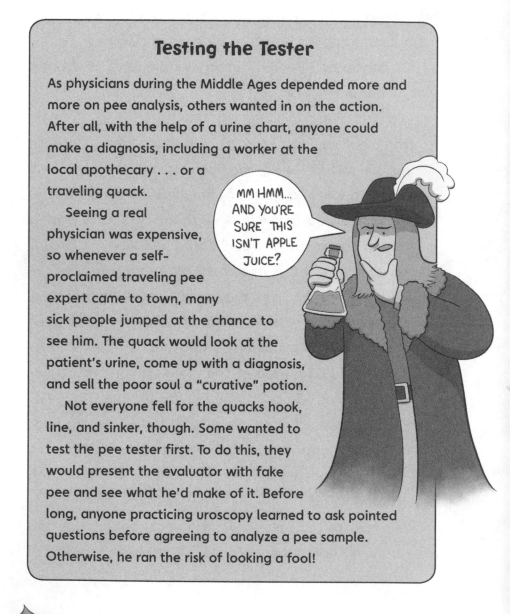

MM HMM... AND YOU'RE SURE THIS ISN'T APPLE JUICE?

Seeing a real physician was expensive, so whenever a self-proclaimed traveling pee expert came to town, many sick people jumped at the chance to see him. The quack would look at the patient's urine, come up with a diagnosis, and sell the poor soul a "curative" potion.

Not everyone fell for the quacks hook, line, and sinker, though. Some wanted to test the pee tester first. To do this, they would present the evaluator with fake pee and see what he'd make of it. Before long, anyone practicing uroscopy learned to ask pointed questions before agreeing to analyze a pee sample. Otherwise, he ran the risk of looking a fool!

Milky pee might mean liver failure. Death was on its way. Reddish pee? That could indicate a fever.

Some physicians didn't even bother to see patients. Or talk to them. Or examine them. All they wanted was their urine. Because, after all, pee told all.

Absurd as this might sound, the physicians of the Middle Ages were correct in one regard. There actually is a disease that can be diagnosed using simple pee-analyzing techniques. And it's all in the tasting: Sipping the yellow stuff can allow a physician to diagnose diabetes.

Diabetes is an awfully serious disease—even today. The main problem in diabetes is that a hormone called insulin stops doing its job. This might be because the person's body stops making insulin, or because the body stops responding to the insulin that's already there. Insulin is in charge of controlling the amount of glucose (sugar) in a person's blood, so diabetes makes a person's blood sugar levels go all out of whack.

As the amount of sugar in the blood goes up and up and up, some of it ends up in the pee. Which means the urine will taste like—you guessed it—sugar.

So when the pee-tasting physicians of ancient Greece and the urine-analyzing doctors of the Middle Ages were taking swigs of pee and discovering it tasted like liquid cotton candy, they were detecting a real disease.

Which is incredible!

Vegetables Really Are Magic

When those urine-analyzing physicians of the Middle Ages assessed pee colors, hopefully they took into account what their patients had been eating. Because what you eat can affect how your urine looks. Eat a bunch of carrots? Your pee could look orange. Gorge yourself on a pan of Grandma's famous rhubarb tarts? Your pee might turn dark brown. Feast on a plate of asparagus? Don't be surprised if your pee gains a greenish tint (and smells peculiar as well). But the most famous pee color transformer of all is . . . the humble beet.

This simple root vegetable has been the cause of countless frantic emergency room visits by people who were convinced death was on its way because they'd started peeing blood. Beets don't affect everyone, but in 10 to 15 percent of people, beet eating will turn their urine pink or red. Actually, beets are doubly magical. They can make a person's poop look bloody as well!

Why not try it for yourself and see whether you're affected. It's as good a reason as any to eat your vegetables.

GUARANTEED SICK DAYS!
2/1$

Unfortunately, though, doctors in the Middle Ages knew practically nothing about diabetes. Insulin itself wouldn't be discovered until 1921. And the recommended treatments of the day—such as eating sour foods—did pretty much squat.

Q: What did the doctor tell her patient as he handed over his pee sample?

A: Don't worry. Urine good hands!

No Taste Buds Required!

Along with doing blood tests, doctors nowadays still look for glucose (sugar) in a person's pee when testing for diabetes. Thankfully for modern-day physicians, however, their taste buds are no longer required to do the test!

. . . . mmmm. . . . .
. . . NORMAL PEE. . .

Urine Therapy: Drinking the Yellow Stuff

By now you know all about how doctors during the Middle Ages sampled urine. But what about everyone else? Don't nonmedical people ever get to drink pee?

Actually, they do. For thousands of years people have been drinking their own pee in the name of health. It's been touted to help with everything from tuberculosis to cancer to asthma to bad skin, and it will even make an appearance in the next chapter in connection with the plague. There are world conferences on urine therapy, and if you look online, you'll find numerous books on the subject.

Ask a physician practicing Western medicine what they think of the idea, though? They'll almost certainly give it a hard pass.

6

Help! It's the Black Death!

Imagine you are locked in your school while a deadly disease sweeps through the halls. It attacks your teachers. Your fellow students. Everyone is at risk—even Lucas with his straight As and Katie with her killer basketball moves. Person after person is getting sick with high fevers and painful boils. They look to be in pure agony. After a few hours or a few days, they die.

How far would you go to keep from getting sick? Would you wear a mask?

Of course!

Would you swallow a pill?

You bet!

But what if someone says the only way to stay healthy is to drink your own pee? Or all you need to do is slurp down the pus oozing out of your dying classmates' boils?

If there was even the slightest chance one of those things could save you from an excruciatingly painful death, would you try them?

There was once a time when much of the world found itself in a similar, terrifying position. Plague after terrible plague swept across Asia, Europe, and Africa—including the one we now refer to as the Black Death. The plagues wiped out entire families. Entire villages. They decimated populations.

Victims of the plague would develop high fevers. Awful headaches. Nausea. They would get huge, painful, pus-filled masses—called buboes—in their necks and armpits and groins. Some even coughed up blood.

Most people who got sick never recovered. The plague was a superbly efficient killing machine.

As you might imagine, everyone was terrified. When the plague appeared, anyone with the means to flee the large cities did so. They raced to the countryside, hoping to escape. Instead they often carried the plague with them, spreading it farther. Within cities and villages, many local governments tried to contain the disease by isolating the sick. They locked them in their homes or in plague houses. Still the disease spread.

Plague Today

Today we don't fear the plague as they did during the days of the Black Death, but it is still around. According to the World Health Organization, there were 2,348 cases of the bubonic plague in Madagascar between August 1 and November 22, 2017! Sadly, 202 people died.

The plague also pops up from time to time in the United States.

Thankfully, the plague can be readily treated . . . as long as it gets diagnosed early enough.

Nowadays we know the plague was an infectious disease caused almost certainly by a bacteria called *Yersinia pestis*. An early course of antibiotics would have brought about a cure.

Back in the 1300s when the Black Death was rearing its ugly head, however, nobody knew what antibiotics were. Heck, they had no clue what bacteria were.

Many people thought the plague came from God. Humankind had become too sinful, too wicked, and God was punishing them for it.

Others thought Jewish people were spreading the plague as a way to wipe out all Christians. This was utter nonsense, of course. Jewish people died from the plague just like everyone else.

Still others blamed the planets. Scholars at the University of Paris—a major center of learning—blamed the Black Death on Jupiter, Mars, and Saturn. Or, to be more precise, they blamed it on how Jupiter, Mars, and Saturn were positioned in the sky at 1:00 P.M. on March 20, 1345. The scholars thought the arrangement of these planets caused evil vapors to come up from within the Earth. Breathing in this bad air is what made a person sick.

Desperate, scared people acted on these theories, not knowing they were wrong. Some folks—known as flagellants—marched from village to village and prayed for God's forgiveness while whipping themselves with spiky whips called scourges. They hoped that hurting themselves would make God lift his punishment.

Those who blamed Jewish people were much worse. They burned to death entire Jewish communities, including children.

And then there were countless ways in which people tried to offset the evil vapors eking up from Earth as a result of the planetary alignment. Most people believed the best way to fight bad air was with good air, so they would walk around with pleasant-smelling substances tied around their necks or held under their noses. Things like ambergris, rose water, musk, and aloe.

Instead of fighting bad air with good air, some chose to fight bad air with bad air. These people did things like hover over toilets or move into the sewers. They hoped the nasty poop fumes would save them. One philosopher supposedly recommended people use "bottled wind" as protection, although exactly how the farts were bottled, and when the butt air was supposed to be released, isn't clear.

Another way people reduced their exposure to bad air was to surround themselves with things they considered to be good poison absorbers—such as toads and spiders, especially large speckled spiders. To do this they would hang dried toads around their necks, or invite as many large speckled spiders into their homes as possible.

Ring Around the Rosie

Ring around the rosie,
Pocket full of posies,
Ashes! Ashes!
We all fall down.

Teachers love shocking their students by explaining how this innocent-sounding nursery rhyme was not written simply to give young children an excuse to dance around in circles before falling to the ground in a fit of giggles. Your own teacher might have told you about its depressing origin. How its words actually refer to the Black Death.

The teacher probably explained how the "ring around the rosie" represented a ringlike rash that came early in the disease. How the "pocket full of posies" referred to the pleasant-smelling flowers people kept around to fight off the bad air. The "ashes" were the ashes of the dead. And "we all fall down" was a cheery way to say everyone was eventually going to die of the disease.

But (and this is a mind-blowing, gasp-worthy "but," so make sure you're sitting down), Your Teacher Was Wrong!

How do we know this? Several reasons. First, the plague did not cause a ringlike rash. Second, no one—not one person from the plague years or a later historian—ever wrote about the song until the 1800s, which was hundreds of years *after* the plague that supposedly inspired it. And the kicker? There was no evidence people even thought to link the nursery rhyme to the plague until after World War II.

So the whole plague–nursery rhyme connection? It's probably a bunch of poppycock.

If you find yourself strangely crushed that "Ring Around the Rosie" doesn't have some sinister backstory, take a few minutes to read up on "The Three Blind Mice" and "Mary, Mary, Quite Contrary." The leading theories about the inspiration behind those nursery rhymes are undeniably disturbing!

All these strategies—from the strange to the murderous—had a specific purpose. They were all aimed at counteracting things wrongly assumed to be causing the plague.

But there were also a whole host of prevention strategies that seemed to come out of nowhere. Like getting Spanish flies to bite a person's thighs.

Or ingesting powdered "unicorn horn"—whatever that was.

Listening to the Planets

The scholars at the University of Paris—the ones who blamed the Black Death on Jupiter, Mars, and Saturn—were not alone in their obsession with the skies. Throughout most of history, people have looked to the stars and planets for answers. Around the time of the Black Death, astrology was a major part of a *medical school* education!

WAIT, WATCH THIS— I'LL MAKE THEM THINK THAT BATHS MAKE THEM SICK!

Doo Hoo Hoo!

48

Or ingesting urine. In fact, many a person who had significant contact with plague victims, such as those in charge of burying the dead, believed they remained plague-free because they drank their own pee every morning. At a plague house in Paris, those tending to the sick would often boil their urine until all that remained were crystals that looked like salt. Every morning they would eat this pee salt on their bread.

But the most disgusting of all the random-appearing prevention strategies were the ones involving the buboes, which were those huge, pus-filled masses that developed in plague victims' necks, armpits, and groins.

One of the bubo strategies was to collect the peelings that came off plague boils . . . and sprinkle them into food and drink. Alternatively, the pus-filled buboes could be cut right out of dead plague victims. After drying them and turning them into a powder, the sick and healthy alike could scarf 'em down. And last but not least, some people apparently got so desperate that they drained pus from buboes and downed it by the spoonful. This would be like eating the pus that burst out of freshly popped zits—if zits were as large as an apple and were located in the armpits and groin. Yum, right?

There is no doubt that the ways people tried to avoid getting the plague seem crazy. Wackadoo. Disgusting. But think back to our initial scenario for a second. The one where a deadly illness was spreading around your school, killing people left and right. And ask yourself this: How far would you go to keep from getting sick?

Q: Why didn't people living through the Black
   Death also worry about the bird flu?
A: Because they knew the bird flu was tweetable!

Chickens Save the Day!

People tried many things to keep from getting the plague, often by striving to avoid taking in bad, poisonous, plague-inducing air. But what did they do when these strategies failed and a person did get sick? They tried to get the poison *out*. They had lots of different tactics:

- Make the patient poop, puke, or bleed.
- Cut open the buboes to let the poisonous pus drain out.
- Apply dead, dried-up, poison-absorbing toads to the buboes to suck up all the badness.
- Apply a chicken. As in a clucking, corn-pecking, tastes-good-when-made-into-nuggets chicken. To try this approach, pluck all the feathers off the butt of a living chicken and press its bare backside up against one of the buboes. In theory the poison will move from the person into the chicken, and the chicken will die. After the chicken goes kaput, acquire another chicken, pluck the feathers off its derriere, and repeat the whole process again. Do this with chicken after chicken after chicken until finally a chicken lives—thus signaling the poison has been completely sucked out.

BAWK?

7

Move Over, Kidney Transplants, Make Way for Poop Transplants

So far, this book has looked at all kinds of people who've eaten poop in hopes that it would make them healthier. There were the Roman charioteers who guzzled wild boar dung to treat their injuries. Ancient Chinese medicine turned to flying squirrel poop when faced with snake bites.

And then there were the Bedouins living in Africa during World War II, who successfully averted dysentery by eating camel droppings.

But nowadays we know poop is jam-packed with bacteria. We know that bacteria cause disease. So you might think we'd have moved past the poop-eating days of old.

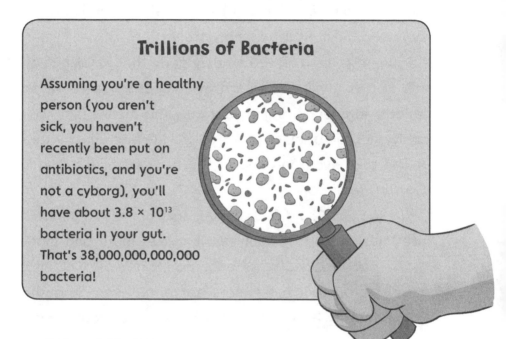

Trillions of Bacteria

Assuming you're a healthy person (you aren't sick, you haven't recently been put on antibiotics, and you're not a cyborg), you'll have about 3.8×10^{13} bacteria in your gut. That's 38,000,000,000,000 bacteria!

But you'd be wrong.

Even today there is a place in medicine for poop. More surprising, it's part of a treatment that actually works!

At this point, I'm sure your brain is scrambling to come up with a disease so terrible, so awful, that it would make a person desperate enough to eat poop in hopes of a cure. The answer: *Clostridium difficile*. Or *C. diff* for short.

The whole problem usually starts with a simple course of antibiotics. Because antibiotics—while rightly praised for their ability to treat your strep throat—also have a dark side. (And no, antibiotics are not secret Sith lords bending the Force to their evil ends.) The dark side of antibiotics is their tendency to kill indiscriminately.

Sure, they'll go after the nasty germ that's making you sick, but they will also kill off millions of innocent—even "good"—bacteria living in your gut. This means that suddenly there is a lot of room for "bad" bacteria to step in and take over. And one of the baddest of the bad is *Clostridium difficile*.

As soon as *C. diff* finds a nice, cozy home in a person's intestines, it starts multiplying. It makes more and more *C. diff* bacteria, and those bacteria make more bacteria, and those bacteria make more bacteria. Before long, the first bacteria have become great-great-great-great-grandpas . . . times a thousand. Even worse, those countless little *C. diff* bacteria begin producing all kinds of nasty toxins. Soon the person develops watery diarrhea. Severe cramping, abdominal pain. Blood in their poop. They get fevers. Nausea. Sometimes *C. diff* can even cause a person's bowels to literally burst open.

Basically, *C. diff* is like the twenty-four-hour stomach flu on steroids.

Most of the time a *C. diff* infection can be treated with an antibiotic. Which, on the surface, sounds odd. Antibiotics caused the *C. diff* infection in the first place, and now we're using antibiotics to fix it? Well, yes. Yes, we are. Except this time around the antibiotic chosen is one that is hopefully a *C. diff*–killing master.

But upward of 25 percent of people with *C. diff* who are put on antibiotics will start feeling better, and then bam! The *C. diff* is back. More watery diarrhea. More abdominal pain. More desperate, mad dashes to the bathroom. So they go on antibiotics again. And again. They try a different antibiotic. No matter what they do, the *C. diff* keeps returning.

Soon life becomes so awful, so *poopy*, that they'd do almost anything to get things back to normal.

That's where poo eating comes in to save the day.

The official medical term for this kind of treatment is fecal microbiota transplantation, or FMT for short. It consists of putting feces from a healthy person into the gut of a sick person. The goal of FMT is for good bacteria in the healthy poop to spread out, take up shop, and get rid of the troublesome *C. diff* once and for all.

And it usually works!

To Antibiotic or Not to Antibiotic, That Is the Question

Thousands of people in the United States die every year because of *C. diff*. What is the best way to make sure you are not one of them? Don't take antibiotics unless they are truly needed! That cold you picked up at school a week ago? Antibiotics will not help. The stomach flu? Antibiotics will not help. A sinus infection or ear infection? There's a good chance it will go away without antibiotics, if given enough time. So while some infections need to be treated with antibiotics—and you should take them if your doctor recommends them!—often you'll be better off doing without.

FMT is still being actively researched, so we don't know exactly what these stool transplants will look like in another ten or twenty years. But currently there are several ways people with *C. diff* can get the healthy "donor" poop where it is supposed to go.

The most direct way is to get the poop inserted right up their butt. Out one butt and in another, so to speak.

Professional Poopers

You may wonder where the poop for the stool transplants comes from. Clogged toilets? Baby diapers? Sewer drains?

Thankfully, none of these options are the case. Often a friend or family member is willing to give up a pile of their poop, and if the poo passes the rigorous screening process . . . down it goes. And if a patient doesn't have anyone willing to donate some stinky stuff? No worries! Because just as some folks donate blood, other folks donate poop.

And they get paid for it!

Right now OpenBiome, a nonprofit stool bank based in Massachusetts, is dishing out $40 per poop deposit. Imagine the glory . . . You could grow up to become a professional pooper!

KRAPPE, SCHITTE, & DIARIA

PROFESSIONAL POoPERS

Address: 444 Butts Boulevard, NJ
Phone: 1-800-123-4567
Email: PoopyDoopy@Butts.csg

Another option is for a long skinny tube to be inserted into the person's nose. One end of the tube gets passed down into the gut while the other end is left sticking out of their nostril. A slurry of poop goes in the nostril end and slips and slides its way down the tube into the stomach.

The final option is that some people will—you guessed it—eat the poop. Although, lucky for them, the feces is usually turned into capsules first. So it's like popping an ibuprofen. Except instead of ibuprofen, they'll be popping some Great-Uncle Albert poo.

Considering how Western medicine is cycling back to poop eating, it almost makes you wonder whether any of the other gross-sounding ideas used in ancient medicine actually worked. Perhaps doctors should start treating cataracts with wolf dung again.

Or maybe not.

 Q: Why don't lobsters donate their poop for poop transplants?
A: Because they're shellfish!

Do-It-Yourself Poop Transplants

If you enjoy reading science magazines or watching science shows on TV, you've probably heard all about the importance of a person's "gut flora"—aka the bacteria, fungi, and viruses that call a person's gut home. Having the wrong mix of bacteria in the intestines is thought to contribute to all kinds of things, from obesity to chronic stomachaches.

Some people respond to these news stories by ingesting more "good" bacteria in the form of yogurt and probiotics. Others take things a step further in their attempt to change their gut flora. A dangerous step further. They perform their own do-it-yourself, at-home poop transplant!

Do a quick internet search, and you'll find all kinds of stories about how a self-performed poo transplant—using poop donated by a neighbor, a child, a parent, a coworker, or a friend—"cured" a person of their digestive problems. There are even a slew of videos showing how to prepare and self-administer the feces. But just because some people are doing this does *not* mean it's safe.

When medical professionals perform fecal transplants, they are super careful; potential donors, even seemingly healthy ones, are often rejected because there are concerns about their medical history. Or because something worrisome is found when their poop is carefully analyzed. Nonmedical people who want to perform a home transplant don't have access to any of these tests. They can't know for sure if a specific pile of dung is safe. It's a giant gamble.

Bottom line: No DIY poop transplants for you!

8

Space Water

Water. We need it to survive. People can live for three weeks without food, but without water? They could be kaput in less than a week.

When thinking about painfully parched people, the first thing that pops into your mind is probably an explorer lost in the middle of the Sahara desert. Or a shipwrecked sailor stranded on a sandy island. Or yourself—that time you had two soccer games in a row and you forgot your water bottle.

But what about the astronauts living on the International Space Station? Where do they get their drinking water as they hurtle through space at more than 17,000 miles per hour some 240 miles above Earth's surface? They don't exactly have easy access to a grocery store, garden hose, babbling brook, or alligator-infested bayou.

One option, of course, is for the drinking water to come from Earth. The space station already gets resupplied with food, equipment, and scientific experiments, so why not send some bottled water along for the ride?

The main problem with this solution is that blasting rockets into space is crazy expensive. And water is heavy. So filling a cargo hold with a bunch of H_2O is a terribly pricey way to go.

Another option? Make drinkable water out of stuff already onboard.

Stuff like pee.

Astronaut pee.

A Bit of Urine Advice, Brought to You by the US Army

Survival 101

If you've read enough survival stories, you've probably encountered at least one where some hopelessly dehydrated person resorts to drinking their own pee. Strangely, some consider pee-drinking to be an important part of any survivalist's toolbox. But is it actually a good idea to drink your urine when you're beyond parched?

According to the army . . . no.

Urine is predominantly water, but it also contains salts and toxins your body is trying to get rid of. The more dehydrated you are, the more concentrated those toxins become. Which means drinking your waste products could potentially make things worse.

This is why the *US Army Survival Manual* lists urine among the things not to drink when you are dehydrated. (The liquid found in fish eyeballs, on the other hand, is perfectly acceptable to slurp up, should you find yourself holding a fish when dehydration sets in.)

Urine Remedies

The *US Army Survival Manual* might consider pee drinking to be a big no-no, but there are some urine uses they do condone. One is for the treatment of heatstroke. The manual says that if a buddy is suffering from heatstroke and there's no cool stream for you to plunge him into, you can "douse the victim with urine." The manual also approves of cleaning open wounds with urine if no water is available.

WELL, I HAVE GOOD NEWS AND BAD NEWS.

The space station has an entire system dedicated to reclaiming water. This system—let's call it the wow-that's-cool-but-I-don't-know-whether-I-would-*actually*-want-to-drink-that-water system (or WTCBIDKWIWAWTDTWS for short)—turns astronaut wastewater into astronaut drinking water. It goes something like this:

- Step 1. Astronaut drinks water.
- Step 2. Astronaut pees. And sweats.
- Step 3. The WTCBIDKWIWAWTDTWS collects all the astronaut H_2O produced in Step 2.
- Step 4. The WTCBIDKWIWAWTDTWS filters out the yucky gunk, kills any germs, and shazam! Nice, clean water!
- Step 5. Astronaut uses the nice, clean water for drinking, rehydrating food, and bathing.
- Step 6. Astronaut pees. And sweats.
- Step 7. The WTCBIDKWIWAWTDTWS collects all the astronaut H_2O, and the whole cycle gets repeated.

Over.
And over.
And over again.
In fact, the WTCBIDKWIWAWTDTWS does such a great job that more than 85 percent of astronaut urine can be

recovered as water. That's awfully good. Good enough, in fact, that instead of "waste not, want not," a particularly parched astronaut may choose to "waste, and want not."

Astronaut Poop

If urine gets turned into drinking water on the International Space Station, the obvious next question is: What happens when an astronaut goes number two? What does it get turned into? While researchers are investigating ways to use astronaut poo to make *food*, they are not there yet. So currently poop gets dumped from the space station in canisters and is sent back toward Earth, where it burns up in the planet's atmosphere.

MAKE A WISH!

Guess what those burning astronaut turds look like to those of us with two feet solidly planted on Earth?

They look like shooting stars!

So that shooting star you wished on last week? Well . . . you might have been wishing on a buttload of stinky astronaut dung!

65

Thanks to the WTCBIDKWIWAWTDTWS, we can all breathe a sigh of relief and stop worrying that our brave astronauts might die of dehydration.

What about those of us living on Earth, though? Apart from our Sahara desert explorer, shipwrecked sailor, and water-bottle-deprived soccer player, one would think water wouldn't be an issue down here on the blue planet. We have rain in the spring and snow in the winter. When you turn on a faucet, water comes out. Heck, a whopping 71 percent of Earth's surface is covered with the wet stuff.

Here's the problem, though: About 97 percent of the water on Earth is found in the oceans. And as anybody who's ever swallowed a mouthful while swimming in the ocean knows, that water is decidedly different from the water coming out of your tap.

Ocean water is s-a-l-t-y!

All that salt means ocean water can't be used in the same way we use fresh water. You can't use it as drinking water. A farmer can't use it to irrigate his fields. And your dad can't use it in his cooking. (Well . . . technically he can, but you sure wouldn't want to taste the end result!)

So while there are areas where summers are full of sprinklers, trips to the pool, and water balloon fights—and water seems to be just about everywhere—this is not the case for everyone.

Hundreds of millions of people *already* don't have access to clean drinking water. And thanks to climate change, the shortage of fresh water will only get worse.

Thankfully, people across the globe are working on solutions. Like encouraging everyone—including you!—to use water more efficiently, finding ways to de-salt (or desalinate, for those of you who like big words) saltwater, and researching better ways to recycle and reuse waste-water. Be sure to read "Where Does *Your* Toilet Water Go?" if you want to learn what this "reuse and recycle" philosophy might someday mean for *your* drinking water!

Q: What can a stinky astronaut on the International Space Station do if the WTCBIDKWIWAWTDTWS is on the fritz?

A: Take a meteor shower!

Where Does *Your* Toilet Water Go?

You now know what happens to toilet water on the International Space Station, but have you ever wondered what happens to all the pee and poop and water *you* flush down the toilet every day? If your house is connected to a city sewer, it probably ends up at your local wastewater treatment plant. Once there, the water gets treated to all kinds of filtering and disinfecting to make it safe for its next stage in life.

What is the "next stage" of life for toilet water? It depends on where you live. In many places the cleaned toilet water gets pumped directly into a nearby river or lake. Try not to think of *that* the next time you go for a swim! In other cities the water is used to irrigate parks, baseball fields, golf courses, and landscaping.

And in some areas of the United States—especially areas prone to drought—new laws allow ultraclean toilet water to be turned into tap water. At the time this book is being written, this kind of water recycling is very rare. But in five years, ten years, fifteen years? Who knows. By that time *your* drinking water might come from a WTCBIDKWIWAWTDTWS. You'll get to feel just like a space station astronaut—without ever leaving the planet!

HMM...TASTES LIKE THE JOHNSONS HAVE BEEN EATING ASPARAGUS AGAIN.

PART 2

YOUR LUNCH BOX

Poop, pee, vomit, and secretions
that people happily
(and not so happily)
gobble up with their lunch

9

Scrumptious Whale Secretions

Picture the menu at your favorite restaurant. Maybe it looks something like this:

- Cheeseburger and french fries: $7.99
- Spaghetti with marinara sauce and garlic bread: $8.99

- Macaroni and cheese: $6.99
- Chicken tenders and french fries: $6.99

Now imagine that squeezed between the mac and cheese and chicken tenders a whole new item has appeared:

- Scrambled eggs seasoned with whale intestinal secretions (ambergris): $500.00

In all likelihood you'd pass on the whole ambergris thing. Pay five hundred buckaroos for the opportunity to gobble up some whale intestinal secretions? Sounds about as appetizing as chomping down on sloth belly button fuzz or taking a swig of gorilla armpit sweat. But there was a time when people would have scrambled to be first in line for some scrambled eggs and ambergris. Just ask Charles II— king of England from 1660 to 1685. He loved the stuff.

Before we get to King Charles II and his dietary choices, let's take a step back and discover what exactly ambergris is. Or what we think ambergris is, since nobody is 100 percent sure.

First of all, ambergris doesn't come from the intestines of any old whale. It comes from the gut of a sperm whale.

Yup. A sperm whale, like Moby Dick. Sperm whales are the largest toothed predator to ever live on Earth, and they're ginormous! A male sperm whale can grow to be over sixty feet long—the length of a T. rex and a half. They also weigh a ton. Well, not *one* ton. They can weigh as much as *fifty* tons. Which is how much thirty-three female hippos stacked on top of one another would weigh.

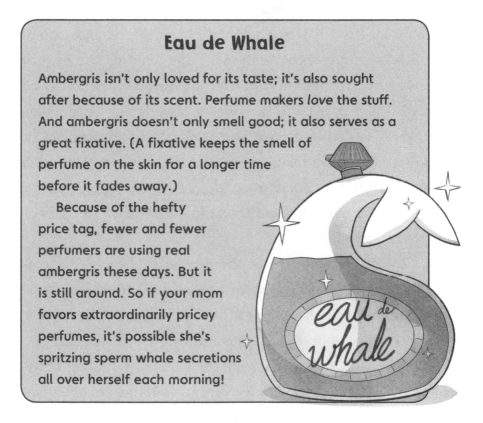

Eau de Whale

Ambergris isn't only loved for its taste; it's also sought after because of its scent. Perfume makers *love* the stuff. And ambergris doesn't only smell good; it also serves as a great fixative. (A fixative keeps the smell of perfume on the skin for a longer time before it fades away.)

Because of the hefty price tag, fewer and fewer perfumers are using real ambergris these days. But it is still around. So if your mom favors extraordinarily pricey perfumes, it's possible she's spritzing sperm whale secretions all over herself each morning!

Because of their size, sperm whales need to eat a lot of food. As in two thousand *pounds* of food *a day*. The bulk of this diet comes in the form of squid.

Unfortunately, eating thousands of squid comes at a price. Most of a squid's body is made up of nice, soft, easy-to-digest squishy stuff, but not all of it. Squid have parrotlike beaks that are hard, sharp, and indigestible. Which means sperm whales have to do something with the thousands of squid beaks they eat.

If I were a sperm whale, I'd arrange for a nice squid-beak spitting contest with my friends, but to the best of my knowledge nobody has ever witnessed a whale dealing with squid beaks the way we deal with our watermelon seeds. Instead, they handle their little squid problem by letting the beaks build up in their stomach over the course of several days . . . and then *blarghhhh!*

The ocean is treated to a big ol' heap of squid-beak whale vomit.

In about 1 percent of sperm whales, however, something goes terribly wrong with operation beak vomit, and it's from these poor whales that ambergris comes from. In these whales, not all the squid beaks are successfully spewed out. Some of the beaks sneak their way past all four of the whale's stomachs and find themselves in the whale's intestines. And this is where the problem begins because—as we've already discussed—the whale can't break down the beaks.

What exactly goes on in the whale gut is unknown,

but some believe the whale's intestines secrete a substance to protect itself from the sharp beaks. And then, over what is probably a period of several years, more and more squid beaks mix with more and more intestinal secretions and more and more whale poop until eventually the whale ends up with a huge, compact, boulderlike mass of beaks and poo and secretions in its intestines.

What happens next?

Some think the whales eventually find a way to regurgitate the ambergris—like a cat hacking up a hair ball. But most experts believe ambergris comes out the other end. The butt end. Some of the whales (hopefully!) manage to poop out the massive beak-y turd, but in others the beak rock gets so big that it eventually ruptures the intestine, killing the poor beast.

After the giant poop boulder escapes the whale's gut, it bobs around in the ocean for years and years. During this time it is exposed to sunlight, saltwater, and powerful waves, and these forces transform the blob from a slimy, black lump smelling of manure into a white mass that smells . . . good.

Eventually it washes up on shore, where the first lucky beachcomber to recognize the boulder as ambergris will strike it rich. Because people will pay a fortune for it.

People like King Charles II—our ambergris and egg aficionado. The king loved his ambergris so much, in fact, that it was rumored to be his favorite dish.

> THE KING DIED AS HE LIVED: FULL OF WHALE POO.

The Death of a King

As we already know, King Charles II loved his ambergris. And when he died at fifty-four years of age, some thought it played a role in his death. This is because one of the theories for why he died (a theory that was, in all likelihood, wrong) was that someone had poisoned his ambergris and eggs!

Cookbooks from King Charles's time include all kinds of recipes featuring ambergris as a flavoring ingredient. It makes an appearance in boiled cream with codlings. And partridge tart. And ambergris-seasoned nightingale. Ambergris even shows up in one of the earliest recipes for ice cream.

Nowadays most people don't go around sprinkling ambergris on their partridge tarts, but here and there an adventurous soul will still eat it—most commonly by adding it to a cup of hot chocolate or mixing it into an alcoholic beverage.

That "adventurous soul" had better have some cash to

spare, though. At the time of this writing, ambergris costs $35 for one teeny, tiny, little gram. Meaning it would cost you $175 to get enough ambergris to equal the weight of a nickel. Or $3,969 to make a Quarter Pounder out of ambergris. And to get a sperm whale's weight of ambergris? Well, that would put you back $1,587,573,000!

It's no wonder ambergris is often called floating gold.

Q: What kind of ink do sperm whales squirt?

A: Whales don't squirt ink. I was just squidding!

Expensive Medicine

Over the years, ambergris has frequently been used for medical purposes. It has been purported to "cure" food poisoning, treat rabies, relieve stomachaches, improve memory, and decrease headaches. It even made a cameo during the Black Death.

THERE WE GO—JUST $10,000.

PHARMACY

Dragon Spit

Throughout history people have loved ambergris. In the Middle East it was burned as incense. During the Middle Ages it was used to ward off disease. And the Sulu people of the Philippines would burn chunks of it to make light for night fishing.

But what did people back then think ambergris was? It must have seemed so strange, so magical, to randomly find the stuff floating in the ocean or washed up on shore.

As it turns out, their explanations were pretty . . . interesting.

The Chinese called ambergris *lung sien hiang*, or "dragon's spittle fragrance," because they thought ambergris was dragon drool that had dribbled into the ocean and hardened.

Others theorized that ambergris was made by bees living near the ocean. Or that it was sea-foam. Some thought it was the droppings of a giant bird. And still others were convinced that ambergris bubbled up from a fountain on the bottom of the ocean floor.

10

Wait! What's in My Candy Corn?

In the world of Halloween candy, little divides us more than candy corn. Some people find the candy repulsive. To them, every piece of candy corn should be tossed in the garbage (right along with those shark bedroom slippers they got for their birthday last year). To others, the little orange, yellow, and white triangles obviously deserve to be at the tip-top of the Halloween candy pedestal. They're nothing short of magic in the mouth.

Most candy corn haters object to either the sugar overload or the waxy texture. You almost never hear someone complain about candy corn because of its shiny coating.

But perhaps this objection should pop up more often. Because believe it or not, the sugary triangles are covered in insect secretions.

And yes. You read that right. *Insect secretions.*

If you've ever bothered to read the ingredient label on a bag of Brach's candy corn, you probably saw "confectioner's glaze" listed. Odds are your eyes slid right past it. Confectioner's glaze sounds almost like confectioners' sugar, after all. And that's just powdered sugar.

But confectioner's glaze (which is also called resinous glaze or shellac) is definitely *not* powdered sugar. It's a fancy name for stuff that's been oozed out of a bug.

Or, if we want to be more specific, it's a fancy name for stuff that's been oozed out of a female lac insect.

To learn more about these bug secretions that candy-corn lovers scarf down each Halloween, first we need to get to know the tiny lac bug a bit better. Lac bugs belong to a family of insects called scale insects, and their life cycle is fascinating. In most scale insects, the immature female insects are known as "crawlers." These little crawlers crawl around in search of a good sap-producing plant on which to settle down and have some kids.

Biblical Insects

The lac insect isn't the only scale insect that makes secretions people eat. The tamarisk manna scale makes a sugary secretion that some believe made an appearance in the Bible.

Exodus—the second book of the Old Testament—tells the story of Moses leading the Israelites out of Egypt, where they'd been enslaved. After escaping the pharaoh's clutches, the Israelites were left to wander in the hot, dry desert. Before long they started to grumble. They were thirsty. They were hungry. They whined that life had been better when they were enslaved. At least they'd had full bellies. In response to these complaints, God told Moses he'd give the Israelites food.

> YOU THINK IF WE PRAYED MORE, HE'D GIVE US FOOD THAT ISN'T HARDENED BUG JUICE?

Come morning, the ground was blanketed with dew. When the dew evaporated, the desert floor was covered in thin flakes. The Israelites gathered up the flakes and gobbled them down.

Some people believe those flakes—called manna—were the secretions of the tamarisk manna scale!

81

Once a crawler finds the perfect place to call her "forever home," she inserts her needlelike mouthparts into the plant and begins feasting on the sap. This might sound like the beginning of a marvelously happy life if it weren't for one little detail. At this point in their development, most species of female scale insects lose their legs! They are permanently attached to that one spot on that one plant for the rest of their insect lives. And you thought being sent to your room for an hour was boring.

Unlike the females, adult male scale insects usually get to keep their legs—and in some species they even get wings. But before you gals start complaining, or you guys start feeling all smug, there is something else you need to know. Adult males can't eat. So even though they get to move around freely throughout their entire adult life, that entire adult life is exceedingly short. They have barely enough time to find some female scale insects and fertilize some eggs before they go kaput.

Getting back to the female lac bugs, they keep on keeping on as they lay eggs and suck up sap. Their bodies modify the sap and excrete it as a super-thick and sticky material. This material eventually hardens to form a protective shell over the bug, her heap of eggs, and the part of the branch she's stuck on.

If enough lac bugs are infesting the same tree, their hardened juices encase entire branches. Harvesters come along and scrape the buggy secretions from the tree and wash off any stuck-on bark, dirt, or creepy-crawly parts.

Whoa, That's a Lot of Insects

Over 150 lac insects can settle on a single square inch of a branch!

QUIT SHOVING!

I LITERALLY CAN'T.

The secretions are now ready to be turned into all kinds of things—including the shiny coating on those precious little candy corn triangles so many of us go nutso for.

Way to Go, Lac Bugs!

A CRAWLING SENSATION OF MAGIC

BUG LAKE

Lac bug secretions don't only appear in food. They are also found in lots of furniture and floor polishes. They can show up in lipsticks and hair sprays. They often coat pills. And you know those strappy ballet shoes ballerinas wear? The ones with the super-pointy tips? Well, lac bug secretions can be used to increase the strength of those shoes!

Now admit it. All you candy corn haters out there are doing a happy dance right about now, aren't you? You're undoubtedly imagining all the names you can call your candy corn–loving pals. Like bug juice eater. Secretion muncher. Lac bug lover.

If this is exactly what you're doing, be careful. Because maybe your about-to-be-insulted, candy corn–loving pals have already read this book. And if they have, they know something you have not yet learned: Insect secretions don't only show up in the shiny coating on candy corn. No way, José. Milk Duds, Whoppers, Junior Mints, Jelly Belly jelly beans. At the time of this writing, all those candies have a shiny coat made out of lac bug juice.

Which probably makes a secretion eater out of you, too!

 Q: What did the baby candy corn call his dad?
A: Pop corn!

Wait! What *Else* Is in My Candy Corn?

Poor candy corn. The little triangles are sure getting a beating in this chapter. Because bug secretions are not their only eyebrow-raising ingredient. They also contain gelatin.

You're probably wondering what the big deal is. It's gelatin that puts the jiggle in Jell-O. It's found in gummy bears and marshmallows. It shows up in Yoplait yogurt, Kellogg's Frosted Mini-Wheats, and tons of medications.

Most of us never stop to think about what gelatin really is. We happily inhale Lucky Charms cereal and Rice Krispies Treats without a second thought. And if you ever did ask about gelatin, you were probably told it came from horse hooves. Which is completely wrong.

So what is gelatin? According to the Gelatin Manufacturers Institute of America handbook, a lot of the gelatin we eat comes from pigskins. The skins are chopped into little pieces, washed, treated with acid, washed again, and then after a bunch of filtering and sterilization and drying and grinding, it's finally considered ready to go into our food. Cattle skins, cow bones, and even fish and chicken are other possible gelatin sources.

So for any strict vegetarians or vegans out there, you might want to add gelatin to your do-not-eat list.

MASHED DISSOLVED PIGSKIN

WILD CHERRY FLAVOR!

The Odoriferous Beaver Butt

Ever wonder why   your cat, Tigger, is always rubbing   his head against you? It's because Tigger has   scent glands on his face. By rubbing against you, he transfers some of his smell onto you, thus claiming *you* as his territory.

Tigger and the other house cats of the world are not alone . . . Scent marking is extremely common throughout the animal kingdom. Some animals scent mark using their urine. Others scent mark using their poop. And some animals have specialized glands created solely for scent marking. Like lemurs, who have scent glands on their wrists and chests. And beavers, who have scent glands located in a more . . . well, interesting part of their anatomy.

Their butts.

Lemur Stink Fights!

Usually when we think of scent marking, we picture animals plastering their scent all over a tree or a bush or a mound of dirt. Ring-tailed lemurs do this, but they don't stop there. Especially during mating season.

When two boy lemurs both want the same girl lemur, they don't put on dances to show off their feet as blue-footed boobies do. And they don't fight each other with their necks like giraffes. And they sure don't create huge patterns in the sand to attract a lady's eye like puffer fish.

Instead, male ring-tailed lemurs have a stink fight!

To prepare for the duel, male lemurs will rub their long tails across their scent glands to coat their fur with the smelly stuff. Then they repeatedly flick their tails at each other—effectively sending stink bombs back and forth. These stink battles continue until one of the lemurs finally backs down. And the other—supposedly—gets the girl.

Thank goodness male members of the human species don't follow the ring-tailed lemur's example. Can you imagine the smell if boys engaged in fart battles to win someone's love?

Right next to the base of their tails, both male and female beavers have two little structures called castor sacs. These castor sacs are filled with a thick, yellowish-brownish, slimy substance called castoreum.

When beavers wish to mark their territory, they build a small pile of mud, twigs, and other debris and rub their butts on it. This rubbing causes the odoriferous castoreum to be transferred from their castor sacs onto the scent mound. And voilà . . . territory marked!

Even though beavers aren't targeting humans with

their scent marking, this sure hasn't stopped people from getting pretty darn excited about beaver butt slime. But why?

A big reason is because of castoreum's taste.

Yes. Its taste!

Beavers: Are They a Mammal? Or a Fish?

This chapter is obviously all about beaver butts. But what about beavers as a whole? Are they a mammal? Or a fish?

I'm sure you're rolling your eyes at that question. Because *of course a beaver is a mammal!* They're warm-blooded. They nurse their young. They have fur. They breathe air.

They're mammal through and through.

And yet back in the eighteenth century, the College of Physicians in Paris reportedly declared them to be fish—based on how well they swim and how fishlike their tails look! This classification allowed Catholics to more guiltlessly eat beaver meat on Fridays during Lent, a time when most practicing Catholics try to avoid eating any meat other than seafood.

YES, I'LL HAVE THE BUCK-TOOTHED FUR FISH

AND HOW WOULD SIR LIKE THAT COOKED?

It's hard to imagine what prompted the first person to try eating beaver butt secretions, but somewhere along the line someone discovered the slime was mighty tasty. Depending on whom you ask, it can taste like vanilla. Or raspberries. Or strawberries.

And what do people do with yummy things? They put them in their food, of course. The US Food and Drug Administration has no issue with this, as it considers castoreum to be "generally recognized as safe." So castoreum has been used as a flavoring in food for more than eighty years.

Before you freak out and start reading all your ingredient labels for "beaver butt" or "castoreum" or "butt slime," I can save you the time. You will not find it. This is for two reasons.

First, getting castoreum from a beaver's castor sac isn't easy (for the person or the beaver). Therefore, according to the 2010 edition of the *Fenaroli's Handbook of Flavor Ingredients*, these days just shy of three hundred pounds of castoreum, castoreum extract, and castoreum liquid are consumed each year. So although it is still found in certain chewing gums, ice creams, puddings, and candies, it has become anything but common. Nowadays, most companies would prefer to use cheaper, easier-to-obtain flavorings.

Mmmm, Is That Beaver Butt I Smell?

Castoreum isn't only sought for its taste. People also seek it out because of its *smell*. The butt secretions apparently have a pleasant, animalistic, leathery scent. If you feel inclined to take a sniff yourself, here are a few things you can try:

1. Livetrap a wild beaver and smell its keister. Beavers were once hunted to near extinction for their fur, meat, and butt slime. Today, though, they are no longer considered endangered in the United States. Which is great for the beavers, and great for your odds of livetrapping one.

2. Nicely ask your local zookeeper to let you take a whiff of one of the zoo beavers. (If you go with this option, be prepared to get some odd looks!)

3. Take a trip to the store and smell some perfume. Although the use of real beaver castoreum in perfume has decreased significantly as companies have switched to cheaper, synthetic versions, some more expensive perfumers still use the real deal in their products.

NO SNIFFING

And second, the FDA allows castoreum to be listed as a "natural flavoring," without any further identification. So if you're lucky enough to favor a brand of vanilla ice cream that does contain beaver butt secretions, you will never know it.

I scream, you scream, we all scream for ice cream!

Q: What did the beaver say to the tree?
A: It's been great gnawing you!

"Natural Flavors" Explained (Not!)

"Natural flavors." When you see those words listed among your fruit snacks' ingredients, you probably find yourself feeling a bit smug. "Natural flavors" sounds so . . . healthy. Doesn't it? It brings to mind images of someone lovingly picking juicy, red, pesticide-free strawberries at their peak of freshness, carefully washing off the dirt and bugs, and gently squeezing all the flavorful "natural" juices out of the berries and into your food. But now that you know beaver butt slime fits under "natural flavors," it's hard not to wonder what else does.

Turns out, most "natural flavors" are created in a lab. They may technically consist of things found in nature, but it's so much more complicated than that. To offer some clarity, here is the US Food and Drug Administration's official definition of a natural flavor. (Just kidding about the whole "clarity" thing. The definition you're about to read—or attempt to read—is even less clear than your math teacher when she tries to explain how to divide fractions.) "The term *natural flavor* or *natural flavoring* means the essential oil, oleoresin, essence or extractive, protein hydrolysate, distillate, or any product of roasting, heating or enzymolysis, which contains the flavoring constituents derived from a spice, fruit or fruit juice, vegetable or vegetable juice, edible yeast, herb, bark, bud, root, leaf or similar plant material, meat, seafood, poultry, eggs, dairy products, or fermentation products thereof, whose significant function in food is flavoring rather than nutritional."

Well, that cleared everything up.

Or rather, it cleared nothing up!

Here is the bottom line: Those "natural flavors" in your fruit snacks? They probably did not get there from someone tenderly squeezing a bunch of strawberries.

12

Hidden Surprises!

Presumably you don't follow Cinderella's example. You don't have a little Jaq and a little Gus skittering around your house gathering corn kernels, stealing beads, and making beautiful ball gowns.

But even if you don't have any free-roaming rodents

exploring your cupboards, you are nonetheless getting the opportunity to sample their scat all the time. Because critter droppings can be found in all kinds of food, such as spices and sesame seeds and popcorn and dates. Even wheat—the main ingredient in most breads, crackers, and cookies—can have rodent poo in it.

That Red Color Is Bug-tastic!

Some insect parts—like fly eggs in your tomato juice and beetle legs in your chocolate—do not need to be listed on ingredient labels. They get to sneak in under the radar. But there is a bug that does show up on labels, albeit also in a sneaky way.

The bug is the cochineal insect, a scale insect like the lac bug, and they get squashed up and added to food to make it red. These bugs are sneaky because finding them on an ingredient label is not as straightforward as looking for "squashed bugs" or "bug food coloring." Instead they're listed as "carmine" or "cochineal extract."

So the next time you read your Yoplait strawberry yogurt label and see carmine, you'll know what you're eating!

Before you grab the phone to alert the authorities, you should know that the Food and Drug Administration already knows about this little poop problem. And it's A-OK with it!

In fact, it has an online handbook specifying how much rodent feces is allowed in different types of food. And unfortunately, critter droppings are not the only gross thing the FDA allows in your food.

You know the peanut butter you're always scarfing down by the spoonful? You'll never guess what's hidden in there.

Right now you're racing to the kitchen to look at the ingredient label on your beloved Skippy, aren't you? Well? What does it say? Peanuts. Salt. Maybe some oil or sugar? What's so bad about that? If that's all that's listed on the label, that's all that's in the jar. Right?

Umm . . . not exactly.

The FDA allows peanut butter to contain up to twenty-nine insect fragments per one hundred grams—which means you could have almost ten insect fragments per PB&J. Rodent hairs are OK, too . . . as long as it averages less than one hair per one hundred grams.

So your precious jar of peanut butter might actually contain peanuts, salt, a collection of cockroach legs, and a smattering of rat hairs. Now that's gross!

And it's still only the beginning. Ground pepper is

considered OK as long as it doesn't average 475 or more insect fragments per fifty grams, which means there can be up to twenty fragments per teaspoon! Canned pineapple passes the test as long as the average mold count isn't 20 percent or more. Frozen spinach can average up to forty-nine aphids per one hundred grams, so a pan of your mom's spinach lasagna could have over 250 aphids in it! Maraschino cherries are given the green light if less than 5 percent of the pieces are maggoty. The list goes on and on.

Astonishing Animal Poop that Doesn't End Up in Your Popcorn

As you've learned, the FDA allows small amounts of animal poop to end up in your food. Like in your popcorn. And cornmeal. And wheat. The animal guilty of making those food-invading turds is typically a little rodent, like a mouse.

But mice are obviously not the only animal that poops. All animals poop. All people poop. It's what we do.

And let's face it: Some animal poops are more interesting than others.

Beaver poop, for example, is interesting because it looks like a bunch of squashed-together wood chips. Which makes sense considering a beaver's diet.

Parrotfish poop is interesting because it's essentially sand. Have you ever walked on one of Hawaii's popular white-sand beaches? If so, you were basically walking all over parrotfish poop!

Bat poo, commonly called bat guano, is interesting not because of how it looks but because of its explosive history. Bat guano is high in nitrogen. The Confederacy used it to make gunpowder during the Civil War.

And certain birds, like storks and vultures, have poop that's interesting because of where it ends up. Most birds poop on the ground, on branches, on cars, or on the head of some poor, unsuspecting person. Storks and vultures, on the other hand, poop on their own legs! This practice is called urohidrosis, and one reason the birds are thought to do this is that it helps them cool down as the liquid in their poop evaporates.

HOOOEY! IF I'D KNOWN IT'D BE THIS HOT, I'D HAVE EATEN MORE.

Of all the poops across the animal kingdom, though, I find wombat poop to be the most fascinating. Wombats, which are cute little marsupials who call Australia home, have poop that doesn't settle for being round or oval. They don't make watery poop like a bird or sandy poop like a parrotfish. That would be way too boring for a wombat.

Instead, wombats poop *cubed* poop! Like little dice!

Thankfully, there's some good news. Just because tomato sauce—assuming it's 100 percent maggot-free—is allowed to have up to twenty-nine fly eggs per one hundred grams doesn't mean the sauce you poured all over your spaghetti noodles last night actually contained that many eggs. Most of the time foods contain significantly less than these limits.

But why, why, why is it OK for there to be any rodent poop in your popcorn, or insect fragments in your bowtie pasta, or pus pockets on your ocean perch?

The answer is simple. Our world is full of bugs. And rodents. And pus pocket–producing fish parasites. So no matter how hard farmers and manufacturers might try, they can't keep everything out.

So yeah. Like it or not, you're eating mouse poo, fly wings, and squirmy little maggots all the time.

If you ever get a hankering to know what all is allowed in your food, you can check out the limits yourself in the FDA's online *Food Defect Levels Handbook*!

Q: What did the peanut butter say to the cockroach leg that was buried in the peanut butter jar?

A: Nothing, silly. Peanut butter can't talk!

Hungry? How About Some Bugs?

Many people in the United States find the idea of insect legs in their peanut butter to be a bit gross. Or maybe a lot gross. But there are parts of the world where bugs commonly appear on the menu.

Like Cambodia, where tarantulas—fried so they're crisp on the outside and ooey-gooey on the inside—are considered a delicacy. And parts of Mexico, where roasted grasshoppers are a popular snack. Or areas of Australia, where witchetty grubs—which supposedly taste a lot like almonds—are happily consumed. The list goes on and on and on.

In these bug-eating parts of the world, bug eating is *not* considered strange. Or gross. Or weird. Rather it's . . . normal.

And as the Earth's population increases and water becomes scarcer, eating bugs might soon become "normal" all across the globe. It's much cheaper and more environmentally friendly to raise a gazillion crickets than it is to raise a cow, after all.

Anyone hungry for some mealworm tacos?

What's That Floating in the Pool?

Sure, there could be hidden mouse turds in your popcorn. And that's utterly disgusting. But if you've ever cannonballed into a public pool and found yourself inhaling a mouthful of water, you've probably also swallowed some hidden *human* poop.

In 2012, the Centers for Disease Control and Prevention looked at the germs in public pools' water filters and found *E. coli* bacteria in 58 percent of them. When you consider that *E. coli* is found in people poo, it's fairly easy to read between the lines and figure out what's going on. Those 58 percent of pools with *E. coli* in them? They were contaminated with good, old-fashioned human dung.

So here's the takeaway: Always shower before you get in the pool, don't swim if you have diarrhea, and never, never, *never* swallow the water!

13

Saliva, Anyone?

Many foods have misleading names. Like buffalo wings, which are obviously not made from the nonexistent wings of buffaloes. And hot dogs, which are 100 percent free of both hot and cold dogs. And let's not forget about ladyfingers. Thank goodness they don't contain any actual chopped-off body parts.

If you have ever heard of a Chinese delicacy called bird's nest soup, you might have assumed that it also had a misleading name.

That assumption would've been wrong. Because bird's nest soup does contain bird nests.

Not the kind of nest made out of twigs or mud or grass, though. No simple robin nests or warbler nests here. The nests starring in bird's nest soup are made out of *saliva*.

I Might Need a Puke Bucket

Because saliva is an animal secretion, bird's nest soup clearly earned its own chapter in this book. But if I were writing a book about the grossest foods of all time—regardless of whether they contained animal poop, pee, vomit, or secretions—bird's nest soup wouldn't be anywhere near my top ten.

Here are some foods that do make my stomach roil just thinking about them:

- Jellied moose nose is eaten in Canada and Alaska. And yes, it really is made out of the nose of a moose.
- Haggis is a popular dish in Scotland. A sheep's heart, liver, and lungs are minced up, mixed with a bunch of other things, packed inside the sheep's stomach, and then boiled.
- Black pudding might sound delish, but this dish—eaten in Africa, Asia, Europe, and the Americas—is made of congealed animal blood!

- In Japan people eat tuna eyeballs. Apparently they taste like octopus.
- Hákarl—basically fermented shark—can be bought in grocery stores throughout Iceland. The shark in question, the Greenland shark, is actually poisonous if eaten fresh. But bury the shark in sand for a few months, hang it up to dry for a few more months, and it's safe for eating. While I've never seen or tasted hákarl myself, it's often described as smelling like urine and tasting like a pungent cheese that's been bathed in ammonia.
- In parts of the United States people enjoy Rocky Mountain oysters. This might sound scrumptious to seafood lovers, but there are actually no oysters in Rocky Mountain oysters. They're deep-fried bull testicles!
- And finally there is Italy's casu marzu. But because casu marzu contains poop, it earns its own chapter (see Chapter 17)!

The birds who make this unusual, highly sought-after saliva are called swiftlets, and they live among the bats in caves found in Southeast Asia. When these little birds want to build a nest, they make a sticky saliva that comes out of their beaks in long, thin strings. Like strands of spaghetti. The birds weave this spit against a cave wall, and before long, the strandy saliva has been transformed into a nest in which they can lay their eggs.

That is, they can lay their eggs in it if they're allowed to keep the nest—because those nests are in great demand. Swiftlet nests are referred to as "white gold" or "the caviar of the East" for a good reason: They're needed to make bird's nest soup, a single bowl of which can cost over $90 in some Hong Kong restaurants!

Supposedly the nests don't have much flavor, and they have a "gelatinous texture," as food writer Ching-He Huang once told the BBC. Despite the super-high price tag and bland taste, the soup remains popular because of per-ceived health benefits. Parents give it to their kids in hopes it will help them grow. Adults eat it for lots of reasons, including to help their skin and improve their breathing. Researchers question whether the soup does any of the things it's touted for, but this hasn't kept the nests from flying off the shelves. Or from flying off cave walls.

Sipping Some Spit

Swiftlet spit might end up in soup, but human spit sometimes ends up in a drink. The drink is called chicha, and it's been enjoyed by people living in the Andes for thousands of years. While the exact makeup of chicha can vary, it's most often made out of maize, or corn.

The traditional way of making the drink begins with chicha makers chewing some maize in their mouths. Their goal? To coat the corn with saliva. Then the maize-saliva mixture is spit into a bowl, filtered, heated up, and allowed to sit and ferment for a while. During this time, the enzymes in the saliva break down the starches in the maize, turning them into sugar.

PToo!
PTooEY!
PToo!

Chicha is actually still made today; there is even a brewery in Delaware that makes and sells the drink!

People have gathered the nests from caves for over a thousand years. Unfortunately for the nest collectors, the swiftlets don't make things easy for them. Instead of building their nests at a nice, convenient five feet off the ground, the swiftlets opt for more dizzying heights. As in three hundred feet high—essentially the height of the Statue of Liberty! To get that high the daredevil nest collectors risk their lives by scaling a bunch of flimsy bamboo scaffolding. One little misstep, one broken bamboo pole, and . . .

Ideally nest gatherers take nests only after the baby birds have already flown the coop. Or before any eggs have been laid, as the birds will usually simply rebuild the nest. But the nests can be sold for so much money that it's superbly tempting for poachers to collect any nest they can find. Even if it contains eggs. Or baby chicks too young to fly.

A Deadly Soup Delicacy

Most people are afraid of something. Heights. Snakes. Airplanes. Roller coasters. A shark attack?

Imagine you're vacationing at a beach. The sun is shining, the air is warm upon your skin, and you're having the time of your life swimming in the ocean. You dive under one wave, then try to jump over the next one. Life is perfect.

And then, out of the corner of your eye, you spot a black triangle streaking through the water in your direction. Your eyes widen as you try to figure out what it is. Your worst fears are soon confirmed: It's a dorsal fin! You've probably just pooped in your swimming suit because that's a shark heading your way.

As scary as this scenario might sound, and as frequent as scenes like this show up in the movies, it's actually exceedingly rare for a shark to attack a human. On average, about six people die each year because of sharks. Meanwhile it's been estimated that humans kill at least 100 *million* sharks a year, possibly almost 300 million. If we go with the lower number, this translates to 11,416 sharks killed each hour, or 190 sharks killed each minute, or three sharks killed every second.

Which means humans kill more sharks in three seconds than sharks kill humans in an entire year!

While some of these sharks are killed by fishing vessels and trophy hunters, many are killed for a soup—shark fin soup—that is considered a delicacy in parts of Asia.

So many sharks have been killed, in fact, that many shark species could be headed toward extinction. Like the scalloped hammerhead shark—with it's cool, mallet-shaped head—which is now considered endangered by the International Union for Conservation of Nature.

As you can imagine, nest collecting has taken a big toll on the swiftlet population. In some caves the number of swiftlets decreased by 80 percent over a span of ten years. In part to protect the birds, and in part to make nest gathering easier, it's become common in Southeast Asia to find buildings that have been purposely built to house wild swiftlets and their saliva.

Only time will tell what will happen to swiftlets if people keep clamoring for bird's nest soup. Hopefully the species will be allowed to thrive in the wild, building nests and raising young for generations and generations to come.

 Q: What happens when a swiftlet egg hears a joke?

A: It cracks up!

Nests Worth Dying For

Collecting swiftlet nests in Southeast Asian caves is exceedingly dangerous. The slightest mishap can lead to death. Astonishingly, though, falling three hundred feet isn't the only danger humans near these caves can face. With the nests going for so much money, guards with automatic weapons often patrol cave entrances. If you try to sneak in, you could find yourself on the receiving end of a bullet. Local fishermen have even been shot after accidentally floating too close to a cave.

Sweet Insect Vomit

At some point in your life—perhaps while reading about beaver butt slime—you've probably thrown up.

Spewed.

Blown chunks.

Tossed your cookies.

And as the entire contents of your stomach barreled past your mouth on its way to freedom, you had the immense pleasure of tasting your own barf.

Now stop for a moment and think. How would you describe the flavor of your puke? Sour? Bitter? Acidic? Or maybe a bit like your aunt Tilly's firecracker chili—especially that time she went a little "crazy" with the spices.

Whatever words you came up with, you probably didn't come up with this one: sweet.

Yet there is one insect that regurgitates all the time . . . and the stuff it brings up is so nice and sugary even Winnie the Pooh would go gaga over it.

The insect I'm talking about is the honeybee. And the stuff it regurgitates? Well . . . it's destined to become honey.

But wait. If your vomit tastes like a rotten fish that's spent the last month floating around in a vat of fermented ketchup, why does sugary goodness come pouring out of honeybees?

We'll get to the answer . . . but first let's get to know our star—the honeybee—a little better.

Honeybees, as it turns out, are incredible little insects. The queen bee might be called the "queen" of the hive, but don't let her name fool you. While she does have an army of worker bees around her all the time—feeding her, grooming her, even cleaning up her poo—her life is definitely not all royal functions, parades, and princess waves. Nope. She's there to lay egg after egg after egg after egg.

Bug Bait

Imagine being covered head to toe in honey. Sounds kind of sweet, doesn't it? Ancient Egyptian Pharaoh Pepi II is rumored to have kept enslaved people around him that were slathered in honey, but life was anything but sweet for them. They were there solely to attract flies and other insects. The idea was simple: If the creepy-crawlies were busy going after the enslaved people and their honey, they'd leave the pharaoh alone!

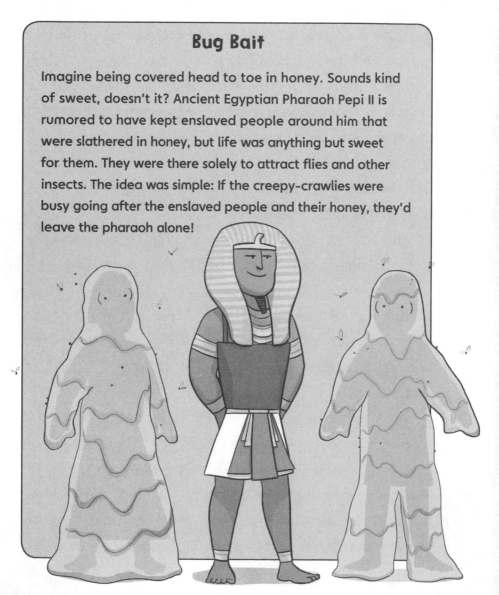

If conditions are right, some say a queen bee can lay over two thousand eggs per day! Considering she'd have to lay an egg every forty-three seconds to reach that quota, there sure wouldn't be much time left for throne sitting.

So who takes care of the hive if the queen is too busy laying eggs? The worker bees, of course.

A worker spends approximately the first eighteen days of her little bee life inside the hive. (All worker bees are female, by the way.) She takes care of the queen, feeds the growing bee larvae, constructs the honeycomb, and turns nectar into honey. Around day nineteen she will finally get to fly outside the hive to guard it. A few days later, she'll graduate to full-fledged field bee status.

Instead of getting a diploma or a huge party, her graduation present is the privilege of spending the rest of her bee life working like a bee. Her wings will beat at more than two hundred times a second as she travels from flower to flower to flower in search of sugary nectar, which she slurps up with her long, strawlike tongue. Once swallowed, the nectar makes its way into her honey stomach.

After she has visited enough flowers to completely fill her honey stomach, she flies back to the hive, where a younger indoor bee will be waiting for her. And now comes the gross part. The field bee will regurgitate the nectar from her honey stomach into the other bee's honey stomach!

Un-bee-lievable Athletes

If you think running the PACER test in gym class is a fitness struggle, consider what honeybees have to do. If a hive is located in an area that's fairly full of nectar-producing flowers, the bees of that hive will need to fly about fifty thousand miles—and tap about two million flowers—to make *one* pound of honey. That would be like flying completely around the Earth.

Twice!

Man. I don't even want to think about how far bees living in a nectar-poor area would need to fly.

(If you can't picture this, imagine the following: You're hanging out at the hive, playing twenty questions with yourself while waiting for your sister to fly home with a full load of nectar. After she arrives, and you've shared a quick "Hey, how are you doing?" "I'm fine, how are you?," she goes and pukes everything in her honey stomach directly into your mouth. And you swallow it!

OK. So let's stop with this disturbing line of thought before anyone actually vomits, and get back to the bees.)

Now that the indoor bee has a full honey stomach, she and her fellow indoor bees can begin the process of turning the nectar into honey. The first thing they do is puke and swallow, puke and swallow, puke and swallow, the nectar over and over and over again. This process mixes the nectar with the enzymes in their honey stomachs, which causes the sugars in the nectar to be changed into the sugars found in honey.

Aristotle Bee Wrong

Aristotle—the famous ancient Greek philosopher—had some curious ideas about bees. And you can read all about them in Book V of his *History of Animals*. For one thing, he thought a beehive was controlled by several kings, not a single queen. He thought that the honeycomb was made from flowers and that beeswax came from the gum of trees. And honey? He didn't think bees actually made honey. Rather, they collected it from dew!

After the puke fest is over, the bees will regurgitate the mixture for the last time—right into a honeycomb. Water is allowed to evaporate, the honeycomb is capped with beeswax, and with the passage of a little time—presto chango—honey!

Bee Healed

Most of us think of honey simply as something yummy to eat, but throughout history it has also been used in medicine. And medical research actually supports honey's use on wounds and burns. Not only might it help a cut heal faster, but it may also prevent the sore from getting infected because bee barf is surprisingly good at killing germs.

This germ-killing property of vomit is only true for *bee* vomit, by the way, so don't get any ideas about repurposing your own puke.

After all that, though, we're still left with the question of why honey tastes sweet while our vomit tastes about as unhoneylike as you can get. The reason for this is our puke comes from our stomach, where partially digested food and stomach acids and sometimes even bile get all mixed together into a stinky mass of gunk. The bee's honey stomach, on the other hand, is separated from the rest of the bee's stomach by a valve. This valve keeps all the stomach acids and partially digested food separate from the nectar. So when the bee regurgitates the contents of its honey stomach, none of that yucky stuff comes with it.

Instead, we're left with insect puke so delicious you may have smeared it on your toast this very morning. And you wouldn't be alone if you did. Cave paintings suggest humans have been collecting bee barf for fifteen thousand years. Which is waaaay before Winnie the Pooh first got his hands, or rather paws, on the stuff!

 Q: How does the queen bee move around her hive?
A: She's throne!

HONEY

IN MEMORIUM:

OEL · SUSAN BEE ANTHONY · BEE ARTHUR · T
BEERUCE LEE · BEELY ELLIOT · BEELY THE K
SSOBEENI · BEERACK OBEEMA · BEE LARSON ·
UTH · BEERITNEY SBEERS · BEELL GATES · B
RS · BUZZ ALDRIN · BEETY WHITE · BE
EEN FRANKLIN · BEEBAR THE BEELA

The Meaning of Life

You know that little bit of honey left on the bottom of your honey jar when you throw it away? The bit that's too much work to scoop out, so you toss it without a second thought? Well consider this: A single bee—working its little bee butt off every day of its life—will only make one twelfth of a teaspoon of honey. Meaning a handful of bees probably gave their lives for that honey you're pitching.

15

Poop Coffee

Many adults—possibly even your parents!—are hope-lessly addicted to coffee. Deprive them of their daily coffee fix and they make Oscar the Grouch seem like a cuddly puppy dog.

Some adults like their coffee plain—with nothing

added. Some dump in so much cream and sugar that it should technically be a dessert. And some crave civet coffee.

What exactly is civet coffee? Well, to put it bluntly, it's poop coffee. Civet poop coffee.

Civets are catlike creatures living in the tropical forests of Asia and Africa. They're omnivores, which means they are more than happy to eat both plants and animals. Their diet consists of things like small reptiles, insects, berries, and . . . (drumroll, please) . . . coffee cherries.

Never heard of coffee cherries? They're the small fruits—usually a bright red color—that contain coffee beans. These coffee beans are roasted and turned into coffee.

Civets love eating the fleshy pulp of coffee cherries, but their guts can't digest the hard coffee beans inside. So when a civet gobbles up a handful of cherries, the beans get treated to a nice, glamorous roller-coaster ride through the civet's digestive tract. They go from mouth to esophagus to stomach to intestines to . . . well, you know what comes next.

Once the coffee beans get squeezed out in a big turd, they're given a quick wash and voilà. You've got a nice pile of coffee beans eagerly waiting to be turned into coffee.

Most people find the thought of drinking poop coffee

to be pretty darn repulsive. If someone tried to hand them a cup? They'd sprint in the other direction like Superman bolting from Kryptonite.

Others truly love the stuff and are willing to pay a slew of money to get their hands on it. Although prices appear to be dropping, civet coffee has long been touted as the "world's most expensive coffee." People have been known to pay $80 for a single cup!

Yup, More Smelly Stuff!

In Chapter 9, we learned that ambergris—aka boulders of sperm whale poop and squid beaks—is loved by perfume makers. In Chapter 11, we learned that people also enjoy castoreum (beaver butt secretions) because of its scent. Well, at the risk of sounding like a broken record, civet secretions are also used to make people smell better.

In their natural state, these secretions—which come from glands located near the civet's backside—apparently smell horrific. Like pee, or poop, or pee and poop mixed together. But take a little of the pasty slime and dilute it in alcohol, and somehow like magic, it takes on a musky, flowery scent!

If you haven't dug through your parents' coffee stash yet, now might be a good time. Look for civet coffee (or kopi luwak, its other name). If you find some, it's time to have a big heart-to-heart with dear old Dad. I mean, think how many video games you could buy if he could kick his poop-coffee habit. If he tells you he *likes* handing over big rolls of cash for the opportunity to drink animal poo, first go out and buy him a few dozen toothbrushes and a gallon-size bottle of mouthwash. Then let him know there are two reasons why he should strongly consider switching to something else.

First, he might be turning over his hard-earned dollars (and letting your video game collection suffer!) for a bunch of civet coffee that's never passed out of a civet's butt in the first place. This is because a lot of civet coffee is nothing more than a super-expensive fake.

The second reason is even more depressing: Life can be downright stinky for the civets.

Traditionally, coffee beans destined to become civet coffee came from wild civets. Free to roam, these civets prowled the coffee plantations during harvest season, searching for delicious, ripe coffee cherries. These civets were happy. Life was good.

Then civet coffee became popular. Suddenly, it was a huge potential moneymaker. Greed took over. So instead of letting the civets roam free, people captured them. Kept them in tiny cages. Force-fed them coffee cherries.

Poops Are a Girl's Best Friend

Not sure you want to *drink* animal droppings? How about wearing them? If you do an internet search for coprolite jewelry, you'll find tons of beautiful masterpieces. With its swirling browns and blacks and reds, polished coprolite can look like a priceless gemstone. But what is it really? It's fossilized animal poo!

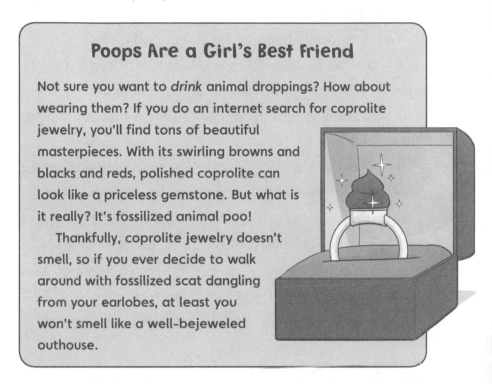

Thankfully, coprolite jewelry doesn't smell, so if you ever decide to walk around with fossilized scat dangling from your earlobes, at least you won't smell like a well-bejeweled outhouse.

It would be like someone confining you to a bathroom for the rest of your life. You'd never be able to run around, feel the sun on your face, or veg out in front of the TV. And that video game collection? It wouldn't get touched again. To make matters even worse, ice cream was all you were ever allowed to eat. Sure, mint chocolate chip would seem mighty tasty on day one. Cookies and cream would still seem like a treat on day two. But after a few days or weeks or months, you'd gladly chuck that rocky road right out the window and never hear the chimes of an ice cream truck again.

That's what life became for the caged civets.

Before you feel too down in the dumps, there is a bright side to this depressing tale. There are people out there who are standing up for the civet. They're advocating for change.

And who knows? You might become the next major civet-saving superhero. Instead of battling the Joker, or Lex Luthor, or Magneto, your archenemy will be anyone who treats civets cruelly. You'll fight to make our world one in which all animals—from swiftlets to hammerhead sharks to civets—are treated with respect.

Move over Superman and Batman. Here comes *you*!

Q: Why doesn't the lady next door like civet
coffee?
A: It isn't her cup of tea!

124

A Twist on Tea

Coffee is not the only drink made from animal scat. Tea can be, too. Like a rare tea made from the droppings of moth caterpillars that have gorged themselves on tea leaves. While this tea—which is primarily consumed in parts of Asia—is clearly not the number one tea in the world, no one can dispute it's number two! Ha-ha. Get it? Number two!

125

Elephant Excrement Extraordinaire

Elephants are huge. OK, so they aren't as big as some of the dinosaurs that roamed our planet millions of years ago. And they are absolutely dwarfed by blue whales, whose tongue alone can weigh as much as an elephant. But elephants are still ginormous, with African elephants being the largest land animal to walk on Earth today.

And being such massive animals, it's no surprise that elephants poop *a lot*. An African elephant, for example, can poop up to 330 pounds daily. Which is the equivalent of pooping out an entire male gorilla every twenty-four hours!

Instead of letting those huge mounds of elephant dung go to waste, some people have found a way to turn the dung into profit.

WHY... IS HE......?

Black Ivory Coffee Company, for example, mixes coffee cherries in with their Thai elephant feed. As with the civets, when the coffee beans come out the elephant's backside, they are cleaned off and turned into coffee. At the time of this writing, thirty-five grams of Black Ivory coffee (about the weight of fifteen Haribo gummy bears) will put you back $100!

There are also several businesses, like the cleverly named Poopoopaper, that turn elephant dung into paper. Although to be fair, Poopoopaper doesn't stop with elephant poo. They also make paper out of cow, horse, moose, panda, and donkey turds! Almost makes you want to take a trip to your local zoo and offer to cart away some of their animal dung, doesn't it?

NO ONE KNOWS.

16

Fly Vomit, Yummy!

 Q: How do you keep a housefly out of the kitchen?
A: Put a pile of manure in the living room!

Most people don't love houseflies. They buzz around your head. They sit on your food. They hang out in garbage cans and swarm around your dog's poop. But if given the choice, you'd probably gladly pick a house-fly over many other kinds of insects. Like a blood-thirsty mosquito, a sting-happy wasp, or a can-live-for-weeks-without-its-head cockroach.

After reading this chapter, though, you might change your mind.

Tasting Tootsies

Houseflies taste with their feet, not their tongues! Can you envision the foot-y chaos that would ensue in cafeterias across the world if humans tasted with their feet as well? And imagine the arguments you could have with your friends over whose sweaty gym socks *tasted* the most rank.

For one thing, when a housefly lands on your peanut butter and jelly sandwich, do you know what it is actually doing there? If you thought it was merely using your food as a place to hang out, or it was simply taking a few nibbles out of your tasty bread, you're in for a nasty surprise.

Houseflies do not have a mouth that functions the way ours does. We bite and chew. Houseflies can't do this. Instead, the housefly uses something called a proboscis to eat (think of a proboscis as a straw with a sponge on the end). They use it to slurp and suck up their dinner. But if you've ever tried to suck up your PB&J with a straw, you undoubtedly struck out big-time. Because straws don't work well with solid foods.

So before the fly can eat your sandwich, first it needs to turn the bread into a liquid. Which it does by regurgitating all over it! Yup . . . it basically vomits all over your sandwich. The digestive enzymes in the fly puke do their thing right on your dinner, turning the solid food into a liquid the fly can slurp up. This means the next time you shoo a fly off your hamburger and think you're good to go, think again. The fly might be gone, but he probably left some nice puddles of fly vomit behind for you to enjoy.

And if eating fly vomit isn't gross enough, think of all the other things that generous fly could have left behind.

Like fly pee and fly poop. (Because flies pee and poop *a lot*—even when they're sitting on your dinner!)

Fly Chompers

Houseflies cannot bite—which is why they were puking all over your PB&J in the first place. So the next time you find yourself swatting at a fly that's just taken a painful nibble out of your arm, the irksome fly is not a housefly.

They're also leaving behind all the gunk hitching a ride on their feet and fuzzy bodies. Like the rotten hamburger meat they feasted on for breakfast. Or the smelly horse manure they slurped up as a snack. And unfortunately, these things aren't just gross; they're also potentially dangerous . . . because they're full of disease-causing germs.

Houseflies have been known to carry at least a hundred different kinds of microorganisms—including various bacteria, viruses, and worms. They can spread *E. coli*, salmonella, cholera, and a whole host of other illnesses. And sadly, housefly-spread diseases can actually kill, especially when they cause diarrhea in infants living in developing countries.

The Deadly Giant Water Bug

Having housefly digestive juices puked all over your dinner is disgusting. Most of us prefer our dinners vomit-free. But there are other insects—like the giant water bug—whose use of digestive enzymes makes a little pile of housefly vomit seem like nothing.

Giant water bugs, which look sort of like a cross between a cockroach and a crab, are giant . . . at least for a bug. Some species can grow to be a whopping four inches long. Water bugs spend most of their time hanging out in the water, often with their butts sticking up in the air so they can breathe. And no, that "butts" was not a typo. Giant water bugs have small strawlike structures on their backsides to help them breathe.

ACHOO!!

BLESS YOU.

While butt breathing might sound funny, the way a giant water bug *eats* certainly does not. The bug uses its viciously clawed front legs to grab hold of its prey, which might be an insect, a fish, a tadpole, a frog, or even a turtle. Once it's got supper firmly in hand, it stabs the poor critter with its sharp, beaky mouth and injects it with enzymes. And just like a housefly's digestive enzymes liquefy your PB&J, the water bug's enzymes liquefy their preys' innards. Which it then slurps up!

So the next time you have a which-insect-is-the-worst debate with your best friend, make sure you throw the trusty old housefly into the mix. Although they don't look as gross as some of their competitors (like earwigs!), it's pretty hard to get worse than an insect that spreads deadly diseases as it pukes, poops, and pees all over your food.

Q: What did one fly say to the other fly?
A: "Hey, is this stool taken?"

Number Two's Number One Fan

Based on the way houseflies swarm around poop, it's obvious they're big fans of the smelly stuff. Are they number two's number one fan, though? No way! Not by a long shot. That title goes to an insect that is so obsessed with all things poo, its very name has dung in it. That insect, of course, is the dung beetle.

The most famous dung beetles are the "rollers." These little critters use their head and legs to turn freshly plopped poop piles into dung balls. Once the beetles have formed their ball, they roll it off to the dung beetle version of the suburbs as fast as their little dung beetle legs can carry them. Why the speed? It's because lazy, I-don't-want-to-toil-away-and-make-my-own-poo-ball dung beetles are often lurking around, searching for already-rolled poop balls to steal. Fights over poop—which often involve one dung beetle sending another dung beetle soaring through the air—are common.

The ultimate goal is to get the poop ball to a safe place underground, where it can be used as beetle food or as a place to lay eggs.

Nowadays most of us look down on the poor dung beetle. And why wouldn't we? Its whole life revolves around *poop*, of all things. But dung beetles didn't always have bottom-of-the-barrel status. Quite the opposite. The ancient Egyptians revered them. Khepri, one of the major ancient Egyptian gods, was even depicted as having the *head* of a dung beetle!

17

Munching Some Maggot Cheese

Off the coast of Italy is the beautiful island of Sardinia. Not only is Sardinia the second-largest island in the Mediterranean Sea, it is also the birthplace of a famous cheese called casu marzu. Never heard of casu marzu? Well, you're in for a real treat. Casu marzu is Sardinian for "rotten cheese," which already makes it sound decidedly unappetizing. But for a reason that will soon become obvious, it's also been given the nickname maggot cheese.

The making of casu marzu starts out innocently enough. Sheep are milked, and their milk is turned into nice, normal wheels of pecorino cheese.

Then things take an unexpected turn.

Instead of trying to keep flies away, cheese flies are encouraged to lay their eggs on the pecorino. Considering a female cheese fly can lay up to five hundred eggs at a go, it doesn't take long before the cheese wheels become fly egg central.

All the Colors of the Cheese Wheel

Putting the Blue in Blue Cheese

Have you ever studied the appearance of a chunk of blue cheese? If so, you probably noticed it was covered in blue splotches and streaks of blue lines. If you've ever wondered what that blue was, you're about to learn the answer.

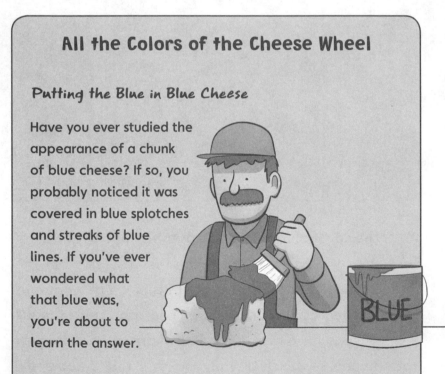

That blue is mold.

Just as mold likes to grow on old bread, rotting fruit, and that container of takeout food your mom put in the fridge and then forgot about for a month (will you ever be able to forget that smell?), mold also loves cheese. In the case of blue cheese, cheese makers *purposely* add the mold. They even go so far as to poke holes in the cheese to make it easier for the mold to spread deep into the cheese wheels.

On the surface, this sounds bizarre. We're used to thinking of mold as being unhealthy. But the mold used in blue cheese is perfectly safe, provided the conditions are right. Best of all, just as maggot poop gives casu marzu a unique flavor, the same is true for the mold in blue cheese. It gives the cheese a distinct, tangy, sharp, and . . . moldy . . . taste.

Putting the Orange in Orange Cheese

Despite what you might assume when wandering down the cheese aisle of your grocery store, cheddar cheese is not naturally orange. It sure would be incredible if cows could produce bright orange milk, but sadly they can't. So the orange in orange cheddar cheese is actually added, usually by mixing in something called annatto. Which comes from the seeds of the achiote (or lipstick) tree.

ORANGE

The eggs typically hatch within a few days, and out come a bunch of hungry larvae. These translucent little maggots happily chow down on the cheese they are living on. And then, as maggots are prone to do, they poop. They chow down on more cheese. And poop. Over and over and over they do this. For two or three months!

As you can imagine, what goes in one end of a maggot is not the same thing as what comes out the other end. So over time, as thousands of larvae eat and poop, eat and poop, eat and poop, the wheel of regular old sheep's milk cheese is changed into something entirely different. It becomes a soft, ooey-gooey, spreadable cheese with a unique, strong, kick-in-the-mouth kind of flavor. If you enjoy the taste of blue cheeses, you might like it (if you can get past the whole maggot poo thing, that is) because casu marzu is said to taste like an absurdly ripe Gorgonzola.

Wait a minute, though. What happens to all the maggots when you eat the cheese?

Here you have a couple of options. If you want to eat the cheese the traditional way, you'll be eating the squirming maggots right along with the cheese. When choosing this route, it might not be a bad idea to close your eyes while eating. Or wear safety goggles. Because those little maggots? They can jump five or six inches in the air. And you sure don't want one of those suckers flying at your eyeballs.

Getting Your Hands on Some Maggot Cheese

After reading all about squirming fly larvae, maggot poop, and holes in your intestines, you're undoubtedly dying to try some casu marzu for yourself. Unfortunately for you, you won't find it at your neighborhood grocery store. Or your local farmer's market. Casu marzu is illegal to import into the United States, and even in the European Union casu marzu falls into a "legal grey area." Which basically means it's a challenge to get your hands on the stuff.

Because there are still traditional cheese makers in Sardinia who make the cheese, the best way to taste some casu marzu might be to try talking your parents into taking a family vacation to Sardinia. To help sell the idea, you can tell your parents that—in addition to being the home of maggot cheese—the island also has breathtaking beaches, mountainous hiking trails, and spectacular caves.

If the thought of eating live, leaping maggots is too much for you, another option is to first put the cheese into a sealed bag to starve the poor larvae of oxygen. A pitter-patter sound like popping popcorn might even serenade you as maggot after maggot launches into the side of the bag.

Before you start contemplating eating some casu marzu yourself, it might be worth knowing that maggot cheese is not casu marzu's only nickname. *Guinness World Records 2009* declared it the "most dangerous cheese." You might think this proclamation was made because of the risk of leaping-maggot-induced eyeball damage, but this wasn't it at all. Instead, it's feared that some of the fly larvae might survive their harrowing journey past the mouth of chomping teeth and through the stomach of churning acids to make it to the land of relative peace and quiet in your intestines. Once there, instead of snacking on some nice sheep's cheese, they'll chew some holes in your intestines. Which can lead to nausea, vomiting, bloody diarrhea, and severe abdominal pain.

Sardinians, who have been eating casu marzu for hundreds of years without having significant problems, don't seem to worry much about intestine-nibbling maggots. And I didn't find any medical evidence to suggest this was a major issue.

But if you ever find yourself eating casu marzu, maybe make sure to chew those maggots really well before swallowing.

Just in case.

Q: What did the maggot tell himself when he got stuck in a wheel of casu marzu cheese?

A: "C'mon, man. Worm your way out!"

Miraculous Maggots

Seeing a wheel of casu marzu cheese, with thousands of wiggling maggots crawling through it, would be enough to send some people sprinting for a bathroom. Because maggots are disgusting. Maggots are gross. Maggots are . . . medical miracles?

Everyone knows that maggots love eating icky things. Like garbage. And horse poop. And rotten meat. And it's the whole eating-rotten-meat thing that makes maggots useful in medicine.

WELL, WE HAVE A CHOICE...

Because when a person gets a wound—like a pressure ulcer or a traumatic injury—sometimes it will not heal. It becomes infected and rotten. It oozes pus. The smell becomes so horrendous, it could make a platypus's stomach roil. (Although, come to think of it, a platypus does not have a stomach. So let's just say it smells *really* bad!)

As the doesn't-want-to-heal wound festers, antibiotic after antibiotic is used; they do nothing. Tons of different wound dressings are tried; none of them work. Even scraping off the rotten flesh (called debridement) doesn't do the trick. The surgeons start talking about cutting off the infected body part. Things sure aren't looking good.

But wait! The doctors have one more idea up their sleeves. Maggots.

Here's how it works: Put some germ-free, medical-grade, creepy-crawly maggots right onto the wound. Let them munch down on all the rotting flesh. Not only will they eat away the yucky stuff, their very presence seems to decrease infection and stimulate the growth of healthy tissue. It's a win, win, win!

This maggot treatment even has an official name: maggot debridement therapy.

AUTHOR'S NOTE

WHILE YOU WERE reading this book, you might have found your-self wondering why a grown-up—and a doctor at that!—would ever decide to write a book about people who scarf up poop and guzzle down pee. I get it. It is a weird topic.

Truth be told, the reason I chose it is quite simple: I find the topic fascinating. I like learning about poop. I like getting grossed out. But getting grossed out about people who eat poop? Even better!

And as fabulous as it was to spend my free time learn-ing everything there is to know about poop, it didn't stop there. I also got to research honeybees, Greek mythol-ogy, sperm whale digestion, and the International Space Station. I learned that houseflies taste with their feet and that "Ring Around the Rosie" didn't actually refer to the plague. As a person who loves learning, having an excuse to read about all these different topics was fantastic.

Also fantastic: the chance to learn about the different foods and medicines people across the globe have ingested at various points in history. To be honest, sometimes a particular item would jump out at me (like a maggot jumping out of casu marzu cheese) as being particularly disgusting. I'd find myself wondering what those people were thinking.

Then I'd remember that I'm from the state of Wisconsin, where we do plenty of strange things. We have a cow chip–throwing festival every year. People go to sporting events wearing huge foam cheese wedges on their heads. We have a city known as the toilet paper capital of the world. We adore deep-fried cheese curds. We fill waffle cones with a bright blue ice cream called Blue Moon. And there are parts of the state where people eat cannibal sandwiches, which are slices of rye bread with raw ground beef spread on top.

And after remembering the many peculiar things about Wisconsin, any tendency toward judgment basically whooshes out the window. Provided animals and people are being treated respectfully, I won't yuck on anyone's yum!

A NOTE ABOUT PRODUCTS

AS FAR AS I know, Skippy is no more likely to contain insect legs and rat hairs than any other brand of peanut butter. I listed Skippy simply because it's what I have in my cupboard.

I also listed several products that contain various ingredients, such as Brach's candy corn, Milk Duds, Whoppers, Junior Mints, and Jelly Belly jelly beans, which contain confectioner's glaze. And Yoplait yogurt, which contains carmine. And Jell-O, Lucky Charms, and Frosted Mini-Wheats and Rice Krispies Treats, which contain gelatin. This information was obtained from ingredient lists found on the products' own websites and is accurate as of July 31, 2019. To be completely clear, though, these are *by no means* the only foods containing these ingredients. Furthermore, because companies frequently tweak recipes, these products may cease to contain these ingredients at some point in the future. I'm not making any personal judgments about any of the foods listed. And thank goodness for that, as I, for one, fall quite squarely into the "I love candy corn" camp!

A SPEWING OF THANKS

DUNG FOR DINNER would never have become a book without the help of so, so many people. I cannot possibly thank everyone, but here are some of the biggies:

- First and foremost, I have to thank my a-m-a-z-i-n-g husband for always being there for me—no matter what. You are my rock. My superman. I love you!

- Thank you to my daughters—Rachel and Sam. You may not approve of my subject matter (*at all!*), and yet you've always cheered me on. To the moon and back, girls. To the moon and back.

- A huge thank-you to my parents (Jan and Don Haasl), brother (Mike Haasl), and sister (Angela Vreeland) for allowing me to grow up in a house where a girl could dream big. You're the best family a person could ask for. (Notice how I used an Oxford comma before your name, Angela? You're welcome!)

- I wouldn't have gotten anywhere without my amazing critique partners. In no particular order, there are the Noodle Friends (Val McCammon, Victor Suthammanont,

Amanda Daly, and Christopher Millay) and the Fictionistas (Cynthia Manocchia, Annie Vihtelic, Sarah Martyn Crowell, Traci Bold, and Katherine Lindsay). Thank you for your honest feedback and unfailing support over the years. My writing is so much better because of each of you!

- Many thanks to research librarian Mark Cullen and the other hard-working librarians at the Verona Public Library for helping me get my hands on book after book after book after book. (And my apologies for asking you to request so many poop books from libraries across the country!)
- Then there are the countless AMAZING people in the publishing world who helped make *Dung for Dinner* a thing. Like Jim McCarthy, my fabulous agent. You're the best ally I could have asked for. My incredible editor, Julia Sooy, who has been *Dung for Dinner*'s greatest champion (and the only person I know who enjoys a good poop pun as much as I do!). There is Sherri Schmidt, copy editor extraordinaire, who fact-checked everything down to how many times per second a honeybee flaps their wings. There's the fantastic art director Liz Dresner and managing editor Jennifer Healey. There is proofreader Susan Bishansky and publicist Cynthia Lliguichuzhca. There is Jie Yang in production and Lucy Del Priore, Katie Halata, Kristen Luby, Melissa Croce, and Cierra Bland in school-library marketing. And then

there are innumerable other people at Macmillan who have played a role in turning my words into a real book. Thank you!

- And last but not least, a ginormous thank-you to the incredibly talented Korwin Briggs. Your illustrations are what bring the words on the page alive. (Actually, come to think of it, a ginormous thank-you doesn't seem like enough. So let's just make that a ginormous thank-you x 1,000!)

SELECTED BIBLIOGRAPHY

CHAPTER 1: TYLENOL À LA BOAR DUNG

Cowell, F. R. *Everyday Life in Ancient Rome*. New York: Putnam, 1961.

Fagan, Garrett G. "Chariot Racing—Ancient Rome's Most Dangerous Sport." The Great Courses Daily. March 13, 2017. thegreatcoursesdaily.com/chariot-racing/.

Harvey, Brian K., ed. *Daily Life in Ancient Rome: A Sourcebook*. Indianapolis: Focus, 2016.

Köhne, Eckart, Cornelia Ewigleben, and Ralph Jackson, eds. *Gladiators and Caesars: The Power of Spectacle in Ancient Rome*. Translated by Anthea Bell. Berkeley: University of California Press, 2000.

Li Shizhen. *Compendium of Materia Medica (Bencao Gangmu)*. Translated by Luo Xiwen. Beijing: Foreign Languages Press, 2003.

McKeown, J. C. *A Cabinet of Roman Curiosities: Strange Tales and Surprising Facts from the World's Greatest Empire*. New York: Oxford University Press, 2010.

Nardo, Don. *Arts, Leisure, and Entertainment: Life of the Ancient Romans*. San Diego: Lucent Books, 2004.

Pliny the Elder. *The Natural History*. Vols. 28 and 30. Translated by John Bostock and H. T. Riley. London: Henry G. Bohn, 1855. Perseus Digital Library. data .perseus.org/citations/urn:cts:latinLit:phi0978.phi001.perseus-eng1:1 .dedication.

Potter, David. *The Victor's Crown: A History of Ancient Sport from Homer to Byzantium*. Oxford: Oxford University Press, 2012.

Shelton, Jo-Ann. *As the Romans Did: A Sourcebook in Roman Social History*. 2nd ed. New York: Oxford University Press, 1998.

CHAPTER 2: EAT POOP TO STOP POOPING

Boas, Adrian J., ed. *The Crusader World*. New York: Routledge, 2016.

Cartwright, Mark. "Albigensian Crusade." *Ancient History Encyclopedia.* Oct. 19, 2018. ancient.eu/Albigensian_Crusade/.

DeSalle, Rob, and Susan Perkins. *Welcome to the Microbiome: Getting to Know the Trillions of Bacteria In, On, and Around You.* New Haven, CT: Yale University Press, 2015.

Flagel, Thomas R. *The History Buff's Guide to the Civil War: The Best, the Worst, the Largest, and the Most Lethal Top Ten Rankings of the Civil War.* Naperville, IL: Cumberland House, 2010.

Flanagan, Deuce. *Everybody Poops 10 Million Pounds: Astounding Fecal Facts from a Day in the City.* Berkeley, CA: Ulysses Press, 2015.

Galli, Mark, and Ted Olsen, eds. *131 Christians Everyone Should Know.* Nashville, TN: Broadman & Holman, 2000.

McElroy, Sydnee, and Justin McElroy. *The Sawbones Book: The Horrifying, Hilarious Road to Modern Medicine.* San Francisco: Weldon Owen, 2018.

Perkins, Susan L., and Rob DeSalle. "Eat Poop and Live!" *Yale University Press Blog,* Jan. 11, 2016. blog.yalebooks.com/2016/01/11/eat-poop-and-live/.

Shaaban, Ahmed. "Now, Camel Waste Is a Source of Electricity." *Khaleej Times.* March 30, 2019. khaleejtimes.com/nation/ras-al-khaimah/now-camel-waste -is-a-source-of-electricity.

Vigliani, Marguerite, and Gale Eaton. *A History of Medicine in 50 Discoveries.* Thomaston, ME: Tilbury House, 2017.

World Health Organization. "Drinking-Water." Fact sheet. June 14, 2019. who.int /en/news-room/fact-sheets/detail/drinking-water.

CHAPTER 3: DOCTORS USED TO TASTE *WHAT*?

Adler, Robert E. *Medical Firsts: From Hippocrates to the Human Genome.* Hoboken, NJ: John Wiley & Sons, 2004.

Bynum, William F. *A Little History of Science.* New Haven, CT: Yale University Press, 2012.

D'Aulaire, Ingri, and Edgar Parin D'Aulaire. *D'Aulaires' Book of Greek Myths.* New York: Delacorte Press, 1962.

Hanson, William. *The Edge of Medicine: The Technology That Will Change Our Lives.* New York: Palgrave Macmillan, 2008.

Lateiner, Donald, and Dimos Spatharas, eds. *The Ancient Emotion of Disgust.* New York: Oxford University Press, 2017.

León, Vicki. *Working IX to V: Orgy Planners, Funeral Clowns, and Other Prized Professions of the Ancient World.* New York: Walker, 2007.

Markel, Howard. "Dec. 14, 1799: The Excruciating Final Hours of President George Washington." PBS NewsHour, Dec. 14, 2014. pbs.org/newshour/updates/dec-14-1799-excruciating-final-hours-president-george-washington/.

McKeown, J. C. *A Cabinet of Ancient Medical Curiosities: Strange Tales and Surprising Facts from the Healing Arts of Greece and Rome*. New York: Oxford University Press, 2017.

MythBusters. "Mini Myth Mayhem." Episode 136. Dec. 28, 2009. dai.ly/x6bkecl.

Newman, David H. *Hippocrates' Shadow: Secrets from the House of Medicine*. New York: Scribner, 2008.

Nuland, Sherwin B. *Doctors: The Biography of Medicine*. 2nd ed. New York: Vintage Books, 1995.

Porter, Roy. *Blood & Guts: A Short History of Medicine*. New York: W. W. Norton, 2003.

Vigliani, Marguerite, and Gale Eaton. *A History of Medicine in 50 Discoveries*. Thomaston, ME: Tilbury House, 2017.

Wootton, David. *Bad Medicine: Doctors Doing Harm Since Hippocrates*. New York: Oxford University Press, 2006.

CHAPTER 4: PEARLY WHITE PEARLY WHITES

Geissberger, Marc. *Esthetic Dentistry in Clinical Practice*. Ames, IA: Wiley-Blackwell, 2010.

Harvey, Brian K., ed. *Daily Life in Ancient Rome: A Sourcebook*. Indianapolis: Focus, 2016.

Koloski-Ostrow, Ann Olga. *The Archaeology of Sanitation in Roman Italy: Toilets, Sewers, and Water Systems*. Chapel Hill: University of North Carolina Press, 2015.

Kumar, Mohi. "From Gunpowder to Teeth Whitener: The Science Behind Historic Uses of Urine." *Smithsonian*, Aug. 20, 2013.

Kwon, So-Ran, Seok-Hoon Ko, and Linda H. Greenwall. *Tooth Whitening in Esthetic Dentistry: Principles and Techniques*. London: Quintessence, 2009.

McKeown, J. C. *A Cabinet of Roman Curiosities: Strange Tales and Surprising Facts from the World's Greatest Empire*. New York: Oxford University Press, 2010.

Perdigão, Jorge, ed. *Tooth Whitening: An Evidence-Based Perspective*. Switzerland: Springer, 2016.

Pliny the Elder. "Remedies for a Tooth-Ache." In *The Natural History*. Vol. 28, *Remedies Derived from Living Creatures*. Translated by John Bostock and H. T. Riley. London: Henry G. Bohn, 1855. Perseus Digital Library. data.perseus.org/citations/urn:cts:latinLit:phi0978.phi001.perseus-eng1:28.1.

Vernon-Sparks, Lisa. "A History of Tooth-Whitening." *Seattle Times*, Nov. 15, 2010.

Wald, Chelsea. "The Secret History of Ancient Toilets." *Nature* 533, no. 7604 (May 26, 2016): 456–458. doi.org/10.1038/533456a.

Wynbrandt, James. *The Excruciating History of Dentistry: Toothsome Tales & Oral Oddities from Babylon to Braces*. New York: St. Martin's, 1998.

CHAPTER 5: SWEET, SWEET PEE

Anderson, Julie, Emm Barnes, and Emma Shackleton. *The Art of Medicine: Over 2,000 Years of Images and Imagination*. Chicago: University of Chicago Press, 2011.

Belofsky, Nathan. *Strange Medicine: A Shocking History of Real Medical Practices Through the Ages*. New York: Penguin, 2013.

Dawson, Ian. *Medicine in the Middle Ages*. New York: Enchanted Lion Books, 2005.

Eknoyan, Garabed. "Looking at the Urine: The Renaissance of an Unbroken Tradition." *American Journal of Kidney Disease* 49, no. 6 (June 2007): 865–872. doi.org/10.1053/j.ajkd.2007.04.003.

Gies, Frances, and Joseph Gies. *Daily Life in Medieval Times: A Vivid, Detailed Account of Birth, Marriage and Death; Food, Clothing and Housing; Love and Labor in Europe of the Middle Ages*. New York: Black Dog & Leventhal, 1990.

González-Crussi, F. *A Short History of Medicine*. New York: Modern Library, 2007.

Harvard Health Publishing. "Urine Color and Odor Changes." Harvard Women's Health Watch. July 13, 2018. health.harvard.edu/diseases-and-conditions/urine-color-and-odor-changes.

Hopkins, Jerry. *Extreme Cuisine: The Weird & Wonderful Foods That People Eat*. Singapore: Periplus, 2004.

McElroy, Sydnee, and Justin McElroy. *The Sawbones Book: The Horrifying, Hilarious Road to Modern Medicine*. San Francisco: Weldon Owen, 2018.

Pickover, Clifford A. *The Medical Book: From Witch Doctors to Robot Surgeons, 250 Milestones in the History of Medicine*. New York: Sterling, 2012.

Robinson, Tony, and David Willcock. *The Worst Jobs in History: Two Thousand Years of Miserable Employment*. London: Pan Books, 2004.

CHAPTER 6: HELP! IT'S THE BLACK DEATH!

Byrne, Joseph P. *Daily Life During the Black Death*. Westport, CT: Greenwood Press, 2006.

Centers for Disease Control and Prevention. "Plague: Maps and Statistics." Nov. 27, 2018. cdc.gov/plague/maps/index.html.

Selected Bibliography

Haviland, David. "15 Most Bizarre Medical Treatments Ever." CBS News. Accessed July 13, 2019. cbsnews.com/pictures/15-most-bizarre-medical-treatments -ever/16/.

Jack, Albert. *Pop Goes the Weasel: The Secret Meanings of Nursery Rhymes.* New York: Perigee, 2008.

Kiple, Kenneth F. *Plague, Pox & Pestilence: Disease in History.* London: Weidenfeld & Nicolson, 1997.

Macdonald, Fiona. *The Plague and Medicine in the Middle Ages.* Milwaukee: World Almanac Library, 2006.

McElroy, Sydnee and Justin McElroy. *The Sawbones Book: The Horrifying, Hilarious Road to Modern Medicine.* San Francisco: Weldon Owen, 2018.

Miller, Nicole L. "The 'Black Death': Dried Toads, Flagellants, and Virginal Urine." *Journal of Urology* 179, no. 4S (April 2008): 313. doi.org/10.1016/S0022 -5347(08)60916-7.

Nohl, Johannes. *The Black Death: A Chronicle of the Plague.* Translated by C. H. Clarke. Yardley, PA: Westholm, 2006. First published 1926 by George Allen & Unwin Ltd. (London).

Phillips, Alice M., ed. "The Black Death: The Plague, 1331–1770." John Martin Rare Book Room, Hardin Library for the Health Sciences, University of Iowa. hosted .lib.uiowa.edu/histmed/plague/.

Rayborn, Tim. *Beethoven's Skull: Dark, Strange, and Fascinating Tales from the World of Classical Music and Beyond.* New York: Skyhorse, 2016.

Streissguth, Thomas, ed. *The Black Death.* San Diego: Greenhaven Press, 2004.

Walker, Julian. *How to Cure the Plague & Other Curious Remedies.* London: British Library, 2013.

World Health Organization. "Revamp of the Plague Detection in Madagascar Yields Quick and Sustainable Wins." March 13, 2018. who.int/csr/disease /plague/laboratory-detection-madagascar/en/.

Ziegler, Philip. *The Black Death.* Wolfeboro Falls, NH: Alan Sutton, 1991.

CHAPTER 7: MOVE OVER, KIDNEY TRANSPLANTS, MAKE WAY FOR *POOP* TRANSPLANTS

Centers for Disease Control and Prevention. "Nearly Half a Million Americans Suffer from *C. difficile* Infections in Single Year." Feb. 2015. cdc.gov/hai/dpks /deadly-diarrhea/dpk-deadly-diarrhea.html.

Kao, Dina, Brandi Roach, Marisela Silva, Paul Beck, Kevin Rioux, Gilaad G. Kaplan, Hsiu-Ju Chang, Stephanie Coward, Karen J. Goodman, Huiping Xu, Karen

Madsen, Andrew Mason, Gane Ka-Shu Wong, Juan Jovel, Jordan Patterson, and Thomas Louie. "Effect of Oral Capsule—vs Colonoscopy—Delivered Fecal Microbiota Transplantation on Recurrent *Clostridium difficile* Infection: A Randomized Clinical Trial." *JAMA* 318, no. 20 (Nov. 28, 2017): 1985–1993. doi.org/10.1001/jama.2017.17077.

Liubakka, Alyssa, and Byron P. Vaughn. "*Clostridium difficile* Infection and Fecal Microbiota Transplant." *AACN Advanced Critical Care* 27, no. 2 (July–September 2016): 324–337.

Sender, Ron, Shai Fuchs, and Ron Milo. "Revised Estimates for the Number of Human and Bacteria Cells in the Body." *PLOS Biology* 14, no. 8 (August 19, 2016): e1002533. doi.org/10.1371/journal.pbio.1002533.

Vigliani, Marguerite, and Gale Eaton. *A History of Medicine in 50 Discoveries.* Thomaston, ME: Tillbury House, 2017.

CHAPTER 8: SPACE WATER

Doubek, James. "Making Space Food with Space Poop." NPR. Feb. 3, 2018. npr.org/sections/thesalt/2018/02/03/582968023/making-space-food-with-space-poop.

Harmon, Daniel, Mary Gauvain, Z. Reisz, Isaac Arthur, and S. Story. "Preference for Tap, Bottled, and Recycled Water: Relations to PTC Taste Sensitivity and Personality." *Appetite* 121 (Nov. 2017): 119–128. doi.org/10.1016/j.appet.2017.10.040.

Harris-Lovett, Sasha, and David Sedlak. "From Toilet to Tap: What Cities Need to Overcome to Make That Happen." *Wall Street Journal.* May 17, 2019. wsj.com/articles/from-toilet-to-tap-what-cities-need-to-do-to-make-it-happen-11558105505.

Lu, Ed. "Watching the World Go By." NASA Earth Observatory. Oct. 22, 2003. earthobservatory.nasa.gov/features/EdLu.

NASA. "How to Recycle Water in Space." June 16, 2017. YouTube video, 2:37.youtube/cR_jQ4Is8t0.

Rainey, Kristine, ed. "Infographic: What Will Happen to Astronaut Scott Kelly's Body During His #YearInSpace?" NASA. Sept. 14, 2015. nasa.gov/mission_pages/station/research/news/infographic_yearinspace.

Sargusingh, Miriam, Molly S. Anderson, James L. Broyan, Ariel V. Macatangay, Jay L. Perry, Walter F. Schneider, Robyn L. Gatens, and Nikzad Toomarian. "NASA Environmental Control and Life Support Technology Development and Maturation for Exploration: 2017 to 2018 Overview." Paper presented at 48th International Conference on Environmental Systems, Albuquerque, New Mexico, July 2018. hdl.handle.net/2346/74153.

Selk, Avi. "NASA Astronaut Reveals the Lows of Space Travel: Packing Poop with Her Hand." *Washington Post,* May 28, 2018. wapo.st/2kx38Ed.

US Department of Defense. *US Army Survival Manual: Field Manual 21-76.* Ravenio Books, 2016.

Williams, Dave, and Loredana Cunti. *To Burp or Not to Burp: A Guide to Your Body in Space.* Toronto: Annick Press, 2016.

CHAPTER 9: SCRUMPTIOUS WHALE SECRETIONS

Aftel, Mandy. *Fragrant: The Secret Life of Scent.* New York: Riverbed Books, 2014.

Byrne, Joseph P. *Daily Life During the Black Death.* Westport, CT: Greenwood Press, 2006.

Dannenfeldt, Karl H. "Ambergris: The Search for Its Origin." *Isis* 73, no. 3 (Sept. 1982): 382–397. doi.org/10.1086/353040.

Ellis, Richard. *The Great Sperm Whale: A Natural History of the Ocean's Most Magnificent and Mysterious Creature.* Lawrence: University Press of Kansas, 2011.

Kemp, Christopher. *Floating Gold: A Natural (and Unnatural) History of Ambergris.* Chicago: University of Chicago Press, 2012.

Moody, Skye. *Washed Up: The Curious Journeys of Flotsam & Jetsam.* Seattle: Sasquatch Books, 2006.

Schaefer, Bernd. *Natural Products in the Chemical Industry.* Translated by David Smith and Bernd Janssen. Heidelberg: Springer, 2014.

CHAPTER 10: WAIT! *WHAT*'S IN MY CANDY CORN?

DeLong, Dwight Moore. "Homopteran." In *Encyclopædia Britannica.* Online edition. March 2, 2014. britannica.com/animal/homopteran.

Gelatin Manufacturers Institute of America. *Gelatin Handbook.* N.p.: Gelatin Manufacturers Institute of America, 2019. gelatin-gmia.com/uploads/1/1/8/4/118450438/gmia_gelatin_manual_2019.pdf.

Hicks, Edward. *Shellac: Its Origin and Applications.* New York: Chemical Publishing, 1961.

Hill, Dennis S. *Agricultural Entomology.* Portland, OR: Timber Press, 1994.

Marren, Peter, and Richard Mabey. *Bugs Britannica.* London: Chatto & Windus, 2010.

Mohanta, J., D. G. Dey, and N. Mohanty. "Studies on Lac Insect (*Kerria lacca*) for Conservation of Biodiversity in Similipal Biosphere Reserve, Odisha,

India." *Journal of Entomology and Zoology Studies* 2, no. 1 (2014): 1–5. entomoljournal.com/archives/2014/vol2issue1/PartA/1-544.pdf.

Omkar, ed. *Industrial Entomology*. Singapore: Springer, 2017.

Piper, Ross. *Pests: A Guide to the World's Most Maligned, Yet Misunderstood Creatures*. Santa Barbara, CA: Greenwood, 2011.

CHAPTER 11: THE ODORIFEROUS BEAVER BUTT

Aftel, Mandy. *Fragrant: The Secret Life of Scent*. New York: Riverbed Books, 2014.

Burdock, G. A. "Safety Assessment of Castoreum Extract as a Food Ingredient." *International Journal of Toxicology* 26, no. 1 (2007): 51–55. doi.org/10.1007/BF00987529.

Burdock, George. A. *Fenaroli's Handbook of Flavor Ingredients*. 6th ed. Boca Raton, FL: CRC Press, 2010.

Duke Lemur Center. "Ring-Tailed Lemur Scent-Marking—And Breeding Season!" Duke University. lemur.duke.edu/ring-tailed-lemur-scent-marking-and-breeding-season/.

Goldman, Jason G. "Once Upon a Time, the Catholic Church Decided That Beavers Were Fish." *Thoughtful Animal* blog. May 23, 2013. *Scientific American*. blogs.scientificamerican.com/thoughtful-animal/once-upon-a-time-the-catholic-church-decided-that-beavers-were-fish/.

Jefferys, Thomas. *The Natural and Civil History of the French Dominions in North and South America*. London: Printed for T. Jefferys, 1760.

Lloyd, John, and John Mitchinson. *The Book of Animal Ignorance: Everything You Think You Know Is Wrong*. New York: Harmony Books, 2007.

Müller-Schwarze, Dietland. *The Beaver: Its Life and Impact*. 2nd ed. Ithaca, NY: Cornell University Press, 2011.

Müller-Schwarze, D., and Susan Heckman. "The Social Role of Scent Marking in Beaver (*Castor canadensis*)." *Journal of Chemical Ecology* 6, no. 1 (Jan. 1980): 81–95. doi.org/10.1007/BF00987529.

US Food and Drug Administration. 21 Code of Federal Regulations. Sections 101.22 and 182.50. July 31, 2019. www.ecfr.gov.

CHAPTER 12: HIDDEN SURPRISES!

Campbell, Michael O'Neal. *Vultures: Their Evolution, Ecology and Conservation*. Boca Raton, FL: CRC Press, 2016.

Caruso, Nick, and Dani Rabaiotti. *True or Poo? The Definitive Field Guide to Filthy Animal Facts and Falsehoods*. New York: Hachette Books, 2018.

Greenfield, Amy Butler. *A Perfect Red: Empire, Espionage, and the Quest for the Color of Desire*. New York: HarperCollins, 2005.

Hamers, Laurel. "Wombats Are the Only Animals Whose Poop Is a Cube: Here's How They Do It." *ScienceNews* 194, no. 12 (Dec. 22, 2018): 4. sciencenews.org /article/how-wombats-poop-cubes.

Jasinski, Laurie E. "Confederate Bat Guano Kiln, New Braunfels." Handbook of Texas Online. Texas State Historical Association. April 24, 2012. tshaonline.org /handbook/online/articles/dkc09.

NOAA. "How Does Sand Form?" National Ocean Service. June 25, 2018. oceanservice.noaa.gov/facts/sand.html.

Padilla, Carmella, and Barbara Anderson, eds. *A Red Like No Other: How Cochineal Colored the World*. New York: Skira Rizzoli, 2015.

US Food and Drug Administration. *Food Defect Levels Handbook*. Sept. 7, 2018. fda.gov/food/ingredients-additives-gras-packaging-guidance-documents -regulatory-information/food-defect-levels-handbook.

Chapter 13: SALIVA, ANYONE?

Boyle, Joe. "Welcome to Indonesia's Bird Nest Soup Factory Town." BBC News. Jan. 27, 2011. bbc.com/news/world-asia-pacific-12274825.

Florida Museum of Natural History. "Yearly Worldwide Shark Attack Summary." International Shark Attack File. Feb. 15, 2019. floridamuseum.ufl.edu/shark -attacks/yearly-worldwide-summary/.

Graham, Benjamin. "Bird's Nest Soup Is More Popular Than Ever, Thanks to Swiftlet House Farms." Audubon, Oct. 23, 2017. audubon.org/news/birds-nest -soup-more-popular-ever-thanks-swiftlet-house-farms.

Hopkins, Jerry. *Extreme Cuisine: The Weird & Wonderful Foods that People Eat*. Singapore: Periplus, 2004.

Hopkins, Jerry. *Strange Foods: Bush Meat, Bats, and Butterflies; An Epicurean Adventure Around the World*. Singapore: Periplus, 1999.

Mugits, Justin. "The Persistence of Chicha." *American Indian* 19, no. 2 (Summer 2018). americanindianmagazine.org/story/persistence-chicha.

National Geographic. "100 Million Sharks Killed Every Year, Study Shows on Eve of International Conference on Shark Protection." May 1, 2013. nationalgeographic.com/people-and-culture/onward/2013/03/01/100-million -sharks-killed-every-year-study-shows-on-eve-of-international-conference -on-shark-protection/.

Rooney, Sarah. "The Deadly Delicacy—Allure of Bird's Nest Soup Endangers

Swiftlet Colonies and Drives Violent Clashes." SFGate, Dec. 19, 2000. sfgate.com /news/article/The-Deadly-Delicacy-Allure-of-bird-s-nest-soup-2720734.php.

Valli, Eric, and Diane Summers. *Shadow Hunters: The Nest Gatherers of Tiger Cave*. Charlottesville, VA: Eastman Kodak Co. Professional Photography Division and Thomasson-Grant, 1990.

Worm, Boris, Brendal Davis, Lisa Kettemer, Christine A. Ward-Paige, Demian Chapman, Michael R. Heithaus, Steven T. Kessel, and Samuel H. Gruber. "Global Catches, Exploitation Rates, and Rebuilding Options for Sharks." *Marine Policy* 40 (2013): 194–204. doi.org/10.1016/j.marpol.2012.12.034.

CHAPTER 14: SWEET INSECT VOMIT

Aristotle. *The History of Animals*. Book V. Translated by D'Arcy Wentworth Thompson. ebooks@Adelaide. ebooks.adelaide.edu.au/a/aristotle/history /book5.html.

Baptiste, Tracey. *The Totally Gross History of Ancient Egypt*. New York: Rosen, 2016.

Buchmann, Stephen, and Banning Repplier. *Letters from the Hive: An Intimate History of Bees, Honey, and Humankind*. New York: Bantam Books, 2005.

Caron, Dewey M., and Lawrence John Connor. *Honey Bee Biology and Beekeeping*. Kalamazoo, MI: Wicwas Press, 2013.

Havenhand, Gloria. *Honey: Nature's Golden Healer*. Richmond Hill, ON: Firefly Books, 2011.

Molan, Peter, and Tanya Rhodes. "Honey: A Biologic Wound Dressing." *Wounds* 27, no. 6 (June 2015): 141–151. woundsresearch.com/article/honey-biologic -wound-dressing.

National Geographic Kids. "10 Facts About Honeybees." natgeokids.com/au /discover/animals/insects/honey-bees/.

Omkar, ed. *Industrial Entomology*. Singapore: Springer, 2017.

Readicker-Henderson, E. *A Short History of the Honey Bee: Humans, Flowers, and Bees in the Eternal Chase for Honey*. Portland, OR: Timber Press, 2009.

Tautz, Jürgen. *The Buzz About Bees: Biology of a Superorganism*. Translated by David C. Sandeman. Berlin: Springer, 2008.

CHAPTER 15: POOP COFFEE

Aftel, Mandy. *Fragrant: The Secret Life of Scent*. New York: Riverbed Books, 2014.

Bale, Rachael. "The Disturbing Secret Behind the World's Most Expensive Coffee."

National Geographic. April 29, 2016. news.nationalgeographic.com/2016/04
/160429-kopi-luwak-captive-civet-coffee-Indonesia/.

Hoffmann, James. *The World Atlas of Coffee: From Beans to Brewing—Coffees
Explored, Explained and Enjoyed.* 2nd ed. London: Mitchell Beazley, 2018.

Jumhawan, Udi, Sastia Prama Putri, Yusianto, Erly Marwani, Takeshi Bamba, and
Eiichiro Fukusaki. "Selection of Discriminant Markers for Authentication of
Asian Palm Civet Coffee (*Kopi Luwak*): A Metabolomics Approach." *Journal of
Agriculture and Food Chemistry* 61, no. 33 (2013): 7994–8001. doi.org/10.1021
/jf401819s.

Winn, Patrick. "It's Time to Put Down the Civet-Poop Coffee." *USA Today.* March
21, 2016. usat.ly/1pEkO1w.

Xu, Lijia, Huimin Pan, Qifang Lei, Wei Xiao, Yong Peng, and Peigen Xiao.
"Insect Tea, a Wonderful Work in the Chinese Tea Culture." *Food Research
International* 53, no. 2 (2013): 629–635. dx.doi.org/10.1016/j.foodres.2013.01
.005.

CHAPTER 16: FLY VOMIT, YUMMY!

Byrne, Marcus, and Helen Lunn. *Dance of the Dung Beetles: Their Role in Our
Changing World.* Johannesburg: Wits University Press, 2019.

Centers for Disease Control and Prevention. "Disease Vectors and Pests." In
Healthy Housing Reference Manual. Atlanta: US Department of Health and
Human Services, 2006. cdc.gov/nceh/publications/books/housing/cha04.htm.

Choi, Charles. "Fact or Fiction? A Cockroach Can Live Without Its Head." *Scientific
American.* March 15, 2007. scientificamerican.com/article/fact-or-fiction
-cockroach-can-live-without-head/.

Frazer, Jennifer. "The Attack of the Giant Water Bug." *Artful Amoeba* blog. Aug.
27, 2013. *Scientific American.* blogs.scientificamerican.com/artful-amoeba
/the-attack-of-the-giant-water-bug/.

Jones, Richard. *House Guests, House Pests: A Natural History of Animals in the
Home.* London: Bloomsbury, 2015.

Learn, Joshua Rapp. "Giant Water Bugs Eat Turtles, Ducklings, and Even Snakes."
National Geographic. April 3, 2019. nationalgeographic.com/animals/2019/04
/giant-water-bugs-ducklings-snakes-predators/.

Marshall, Stephen A. *Flies: The Natural History and Diversity of Diptera.* Buffalo,
NY: Firefly Books, 2012.

Milne, Lorus Johnson, and Margery Milne. *National Audubon Society Field Guide
to Insects and Spiders: North America.* New York: Alfred A. Knopf, 1980.

Piper, Ross. *Pests: A Guide to the World's Most Maligned, Yet Misunderstood Creatures.* Santa Barbara, CA: Greenwood, 2011.

Resh, Vincent H., and Ring T. Cardé, eds. *Encyclopedia of Insects.* San Diego: Academic Press, 2003.

San Diego Zoo. "Dung Beetle." animals.sandiegozoo.org/animals/dung-beetle.

CHAPTER 17: MUNCHING SOME MAGGOT CHEESE

Caruso, Nick, and Dani Rabaiotti. *True or Poo? The Definitive Field Guide to Filthy Animal Facts and Falsehoods.* New York: Hachette Books, 2018.

Donnelly, Catherine, ed. *The Oxford Companion to Cheese.* New York: Oxford University Press, 2016.

Dorn, Lori. "How the Rare Traditional Sardinian Delicacy of Maggot Fermented Sheep Cheese Is Made." *Laughing Squid* blog. Jan. 3, 2019. laughingsquid .com/how-maggot-fermented-sheep-cheese-is-made/.

Europe Direct Contact Centre, email message to author, May 9, 2019.

Herz, Rachel. *That's Disgusting: Unraveling the Mysteries of Repulsion.* New York: W. W. Norton, 2012.

Lewis, Caitlin, and Phillip E. Kaufman. "Cheese Skipper, Ham Skipper." Featured Creatures. University of Florida Entomology and Nematology Department. Nov. 2018. entnemdept.ufl.edu/Creatures/urban/flies/cheese_skipper.htm.

Scotter, Michael J., ed. *Colour Additives for Foods and Beverages.* Cambridge, UK: Woodhead, 2015.

Sherman, Ronald A. "Maggot Therapy Takes Us Back to the Future of Wound Care: New and Improved Maggot Therapy for the 21st Century." *Journal of Diabetes Science and Technology* 3, no. 2 (March 2009): 336–344. doi.org/10 .1177/193229680900300215.

Tunick, Michael H. *The Science of Cheese.* New York: Oxford University Press, 2014.

INDEX

Index

Index

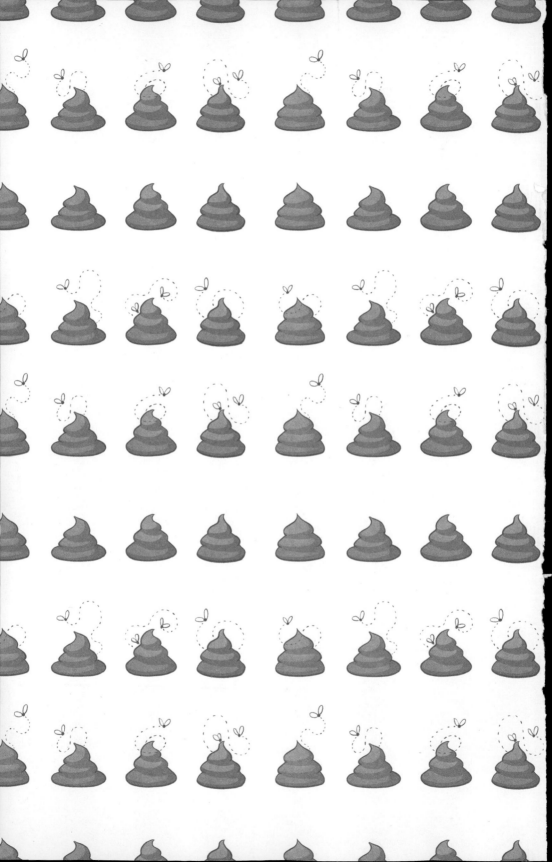